THE
GENUINE
GROUND
OF
ONENESS

Witness Lee

Living Stream Ministry
Anaheim, CA • www.lsm.org

First Edition, December 1979.

ISBN 978-0-87083-022-8

Published by

Living Stream Ministry
2431 W. La Palma Ave., Anaheim, CA 92801 U.S.A.
P. O. Box 2121, Anaheim, CA 92814 U.S.A.

Printed in the United States of America

17 18 19 20 21 / 14 13 12 11 10

CONTENTS

PREFACE

This book is composed of messages given by Brother Witness Lee in August 1979 in Anaheim, California.

CHAPTER ONE

ONENESS IN THE FOUR GREAT ACTS OF GOD

Scripture Reading: Gen. 1:26; 2:8-9, 16-17, 22; 12:1-2; Matt. 16:16-19; Eph. 1:22-23; 3:9-11, 21; 4:4-6, 11-12; 5:25-27; Col. 3:10-11; Rev. 21:2-3; 22:1-2

Whenever we speak about the ground of the church, we find ourselves engaged in spiritual warfare. Satan, the enemy of God, hates this matter of the church ground, which has been concealed from the Lord's people for centuries. The ground of the church is directly related to the importance of the church. Certain portions of the Word, such as Matthew, Ephesians, and Revelation, reveal the importance of the church. Let us first consider the importance of the church as shown in these books. Then we will go on to consider the inward and outward aspects of the church. This will prepare us to appreciate the oneness manifested in the four great acts of God.

PLANNED IN ETERNITY PAST

In Ephesians, a book on the church, we see that the church was planned by God in eternity past. According to the desire of His heart, God planned before time began to have the church. Hence, the church is according to God's eternal purpose, according to the eternal plan of God. Although the church came into existence in time, it was planned by God in eternity.

Not many Christians today have a serious regard for the church. They tend to take the church for granted and concentrate on matters such as salvation, holiness, victory, and spirituality. When Christians do speak of the church, it is often in the way of debating or criticizing. Very few believers pay attention to the church in a positive way. Many seeking Christians consider it a waste of time to devote their attention to the church. Nevertheless, in the book of Ephesians we see that the church is related to God's will and to the desire of God's heart. Since the church is such a great matter in the eyes of God, we dare not take it lightly.

THE BODY, THE FULLNESS OF CHRIST

Ephesians also reveals that the church is the Body, "the fullness of the One who fills all in all" (1:23). The church is the Body, the fullness, of the all-inclusive, infinite, unlimited Christ. How great the church is! It is not a mere association or religious organization. The church is the very Body of Christ. Just as we need a physical body through which to express ourselves, so the infinite and unlimited Christ needs a Body as His fullness in order that He may be expressed in the universe. Certainly this is far more important than personal salvation or spirituality. If we see that the church is the Body, the fullness, of the all-inclusive Christ, we will never again regard it as an insignificant matter.

THE GOAL OF CHRIST'S DEATH

In Ephesians 5:25 Paul says that Christ "loved the church and gave Himself up for her." This indicates that when Christ died on the cross, He gave Himself up for the church. The goal of His death was the producing of the church. When we were saved, we realized that Christ loved us and died for us. There is, of course, nothing wrong with this realization. However, we also need to see that Christ loved us and died for us so that we could be part of the church. Ultimately, He loved the church and died in order to produce the church. Christ's love manifested in His death on the cross had a definite goal. This goal is not to have millions of individual believers; it is to have the church. Christ loves us for the sake of the church. He loved us and died for us so that we may be members of His Body, the church.

THE PURPOSE OF THE GIFTS

Ephesians 4:11 and 12 say that Christ "gave some as apostles and some as prophets and some as evangelists and some as shepherds and teachers, for the perfecting of the saints unto the work of the ministry, unto the building up of the Body of Christ." Christ has not presented such gifts to the church for the purpose of accomplishing a work of evangelism, Bible teaching, or edification. All these gifts have been given for the purpose of perfecting the saints for the building up of the Body. The apostles, prophets, evangelists, and shepherds and teachers have been given with a view to one goal: to perfect the saints for the building up of the church. However, in much of today's Christian work and activity the church is neglected. Therefore, we need to be impressed with the importance of the church. According to Ephesians, God's purpose is related to the church, and He has given all the gifts for the building up of the church.

BECOMING SONS FOR THE BODY

Matthew 16 also indicates the importance of the church. In verse 15 the Lord asked His disciples, "Who do you say that I am?" Peter took the lead to answer, "You are the Christ, the Son of the living God" (v. 16). Peter received the revelation that Jesus was the Christ, the One appointed by God to accomplish God's commission. No doubt, this commission is related to the building up of the church. Peter saw that the Lord Jesus was both the Christ and the Son of the living God. As the Son of the living God, the Lord produces the many sons of God who are the members of the Body. The Body of Christ cannot be built with the natural man. On the contrary, His Body can be built only with those who have been regenerated to become sons of God.

When we believed in the Lord Jesus, we received Him as the Son of the living God, not only as the Savior and the Redeemer. Most Christians realize that at the time they were saved they received Christ as the Savior and Redeemer, but not many realize that they also received Him as the Son of the living God. When I was converted to Christ, I did not have this realization. Our Savior, Jesus Christ, is the Son of the living God. The significance of this title of Christ is that He is the One who makes us sons of God. Through receiving Christ as the Son of God, we also have become sons of God.

According to the book of Romans, all those who have been justified through faith in Christ are members of the Body of Christ. However, in order to be members of the Body, we must first become sons of God; that is, we must first be "sonized."

For this reason, sonship is mentioned in chapter 8 of Romans, whereas the Body is mentioned in chapter 12. Only through becoming sons of God can we become members of the Body of Christ.

FOR THE BUILDING UP OF THE CHURCH

Peter was blessed to see the revelation that Jesus is the One anointed to carry out God's commission and also the Son of God to produce the many sons of God to be members of the Body, the church. As soon as Peter declared that Jesus was the Christ, the Son of the living God, the Lord went on to speak concerning the building up of His church: "I also say to you that you are Peter, and upon this rock I will build My church" (Matt. 16:18). This indicates that whatever Christ is, is for the building up of the church. Not only is Christ's death for the church, but He Himself, His very person with all His qualifications, titles, and offices, is also for the building up of the church.

TWO REALMS

Moreover, the Lord Jesus told Peter that the gates of Hades would not prevail against the builded church. The church affects the gates of Hades. In verse 19 the Lord Jesus spoke of the keys of the kingdom of the heavens. The gates of Hades refer to the realm of Satan's power, whereas the kingdom of the heavens refers to the realm of God's rule. Here we have two realms: the hellish realm of Satan's power and the heavenly realm of God's kingdom. The church has much to do with these two realms. Satan, the subtle one, is filled with hatred when God's children care for the church. He realizes that the church is able to deal with the gates of Hades. He knows that the gates of Hades cannot prevail against the church built by Christ upon the rock, which refers both to Christ Himself and to the revelation concerning Christ given by the Father to Peter. The Lord Jesus did not say that the gates of Hades would not prevail against the millions of Christians saved through Him. Individualistic believers are no threat to the enemy. However, when believers come together to be the church, Satan trembles, and the gates of Hades are threatened.

The Lord's word here implies that as He is building up the

church, the gates of Hades will rise up against it. But they cannot prevail against the church built by Christ. The word *prevail* implies warfare. As the building of the church is taking place, a war is raging. Nevertheless, in this warfare the gates of Hades cannot prevail against the church.

Before the Lord's recovery came to this country, there was none of the kind of spiritual warfare that we see today. We in the recovery are small in number, especially compared to the Roman Catholic Church and the major denominations. Although we are small and seemingly insignificant, we are fiercely attacked and opposed. Behind this attack and opposition is the power of Satan, the gates of Hades. Before the Lord began to recover the church life in this country, the power of darkness could afford to be at rest. But now that the Lord is in the process of building up the proper church life, this power rises up against the church. But the church has the keys of the kingdom of the heavens, and these keys will prevail over the gates of Hades.

The conflict between the church and the gates of Hades is a further indication of the importance of the church. Wherever the church is, there the gates of Hades cannot prevail, for there the kingdom of the heavens is powerful and prevailing. In the church the keys of the kingdom work in power.

THE TESTIMONY OF JESUS

In Revelation, as the last book of the New Testament, the importance of the church is stressed even more as the testimony of Jesus in each locality. Every local church is a lampstand shining out Christ. Without a proper local church, the testimony of Jesus could never be practical and prevailing.

THE INWARD AND OUTWARD ASPECTS
OF THE CHURCH

Having seen the importance of the church, we now come to the inward and outward aspects of the church. According to God's ordained principle, virtually everything in the universe has two aspects—an inward aspect related to the content and an outward aspect related to the appearance. This is also true of the church. The inward aspect of the church is the content of the church and is related to the church's testimony. The outward aspect of the church is related to the ground of the church, to the church's appearance. The content of the church is the church's testimony, but the appearance of the church is the church's ground. Many so-called spiritual believers care only for the content of the church, the testimony, but not at all for the ground of the church. However, it is ridiculous to care for the one aspect and neglect the other. We should have a high regard for both the content of the church and the ground of the church.

Our very existence as human beings testifies that we must care for both aspects. As humans, we have an inward aspect—our soul and spirit—and an outward aspect as well—our body. Although we very much appreciate our spirit and our soul, we also devote a great deal of attention to the care of our physical body. Actually, most of the things in our culture are designed for the care of man's physical existence. We dare not minimize the importance of the outward aspect of human life.

THE IMPORTANCE OF THE GROUND OF THE CHURCH

Although we can easily see the importance of the outward aspect of man's life, we may not see the importance of the outward aspect of the church. Some so-called spiritual people actually ignore the ground of the church. They may even claim that this aspect of the church is unimportant or unnecessary. They may realize that to touch this aspect of the church can cause problems. In dealing with spirituality or with the spiritual testimony of the church, on the contrary, the problems may be fewer. But when we come to the outward aspect of the church, to the ground of the church, many problems arise. This is the reason that those who pursue spirituality often attempt to avoid the matter of the ground of the church. Nevertheless, just as we care for our physical body in order to maintain our existence, so we must also take care of the ground of the church in order to practice the proper church life. Apart from the ground of the church, there is no way for the church to exist in a practical way. Because the ground of the church is neglected, there is no practical expression of the church in today's Christianity. By this we see that the matter of the church ground is extremely crucial.

More than fifty years ago in China, the Lord raised up a group of young Christians and brought them into His recovery. As the years went by, we gradually came to see the ground of the church. However, it was not until 1937, when Brother Nee delivered the messages printed in *The Normal Christian Church Life,* that we clearly saw the importance of the church ground. Now, by the Lord's mercy, this matter has been made crystal clear to us.

The question of the ground of the church exposes the seriousness of division. Whenever we come to the church ground, we must be prepared to face the problem of division. As we all know, today there are hundreds of divisions among Christians. These divisions are all related to the neglect of the ground of the church, not to the content or testimony of the church.

The ground of the church is the oneness of the church. When we have oneness, we have the ground. But if we lose the genuine oneness, we also lose the ground. Hence, to speak of the ground of the church, it is necessary for us to see the oneness of the church. This oneness is a great truth in the Scriptures.

THE ONENESS OF GOD IN CREATION

The Bible reveals four great acts, or activities, of God: creation, selection, the new creation, and the New Jerusalem. In each of these four acts we see the matter of oneness. The first three actions—the creation, the selection of the nation of Israel, and the formation of the church as the new creation—have already taken place. The coming of the New Jerusalem, God's new city, of course, will take place in the future. After the age of the millennium, this new city will be manifested in full.

God's creation was uniquely one. He did not create more than one universe. Furthermore, in this unique universe, man is the focal point of God's creation. The Bible clearly reveals that God created just one man. When I was young, I wondered why God did not create billions of people at the same time. It seemed to me that it would have been much wiser for God to carry on the work of creation in this way. To be sure, God was able to simultaneously create billions of human beings. However, He did not do so. For the sake of the oneness, God created one man, Adam.

Genesis 1:26 says, "God said, Let Us make man in Our image, according to Our likeness; and let them have dominion." According to this verse, God first said, "Let Us make man." Then He went on to say, "Let them have dominion." In referring to the man created in His image, God used a plural pronoun. This indicates that the one man created by God was a corporate man. God's intention is not to have many men; it is to have one corporate man. This is for the keeping of the oneness.

This principle applies to the church today. On the one hand, with reference to the church, we may speak of the church in a particular locality, such as the church in Anaheim. But, on the other hand, we may also refer to the church by using such pronouns as *we* and *us* to denote the members of the church. Because the church is a corporate entity, it includes all the believers in a locality. Therefore, in referring to the church, we may speak either of the church in singular number or of us, the believers in Christ, in plural number. This means that the church is a corporate entity and that we are the church. Just as the church is a corporate entity, so, in the same principle, the man created by God was a corporate man.

THE ONENESS OF GOD IN SELECTION

However, due to the repeated falls of man, the corporate man created by God became fallen. Step by step the man created for God's purpose fell lower and lower until, with the lowest stage of his fall at Babel, he was divided into nations. The one man was of God, but the many nations had their source in the devil. The nations were devilish because they were divisions of the corporate man created by God for the fulfillment of His purpose. When this corporate man became the nations, it was no longer possible for him to carry out God's purpose. At that point, God was forced to give up fallen mankind. Therefore, for the sake of His eternal purpose, God came in to call out one man, Abraham, to be the father of the called race. He selected one person from among fallen mankind to be the father of the called race. Just as God had created one man, so He called only one man. We may think that God should have called out a multitude of people. If we were God at the time of the calling of Abraham, we certainly would have called many people. However, it would have been against God's nature to call more than one person. God's nature is oneness. Hence, both in creation and in selection He was true to His nature. When Paul speaks of the oneness of the church in Ephesians 4, he speaks of one Spirit, one Lord, and one God. Because God is uniquely one, He is bound by His nature to create one man and also to call one man. To act otherwise would be contrary to His nature.

God does not act hastily. Although He is the almighty God, He never does anything in a hasty way. He created one man, Adam, and He selected one man, Abraham. Because His nature is oneness, He created only one person and called only one person.

When the descendants of Abraham were about to enter into the good land, God charged them not to worship at the place of their choice (Deut. 12:8). Rather, they were required to go to the place of God's choice, to the place He had chosen to put His name for His habitation (v. 5). No matter how many Israelites there might have been, they were required to come to this unique place three times a year. According to the natural concept, such a requirement is not reasonable. Nevertheless, God required this of His people in order to keep the oneness. However, the oneness of God's people was eventually lost. First, the oneness of created mankind was damaged. Furthermore, due to the degradation of the nation of Israel, the oneness of God's chosen people was also destroyed. Some were carried off to Assyria, others to Egypt, and still more to Babylon. Such a division of God's people was a frustration to the fulfillment of His purpose.

THE ONENESS OF GOD IN THE NEW CREATION

In producing the church as the new creation, God also acted according to His nature of oneness. How many churches were produced on the day of Pentecost? The answer, as we all know, is that at Pentecost just one church came into existence. The Lord Jesus lived on earth for thirty-three and a half years. At the end of these years He did not have, as we might expect, millions of followers. He had not established schools for the training of disciples. During the years of His ministry, the Lord had miraculously fed a multitude of people on at least two occasions. However, He apparently did nothing to retain a large following. Therefore, on the day of Pentecost only one hundred twenty were meeting together.

Once again we see that God's way is the way of oneness. For this reason, only one church was produced on the day of Pentecost, the day that marked the beginning of the church life. This indicates that the beginning of the church was in the unique oneness that is according to the nature of God. The many churches that later came into existence through the expansion of the church life may be compared to the descendants of Adam and Abraham. Although Adam has had countless descendants, the fact remains that in God's creation there was just one man. In like manner, although Abraham's descendants were to be as the sand of the seashore, God nonetheless originally called just one person. Now in the New Testament we see that on the day of Pentecost only one church was produced by the Spirit. This church is the Body and also the one new man.

As the new man, the church is a corporate man, just as Adam was a corporate man. Furthermore, as the corporate man of God's creation was divided into nations, so the corporate man of God's new creation has been divided into denominations. This is the work of Satan. The nations damaged the one man of God's creation, and the denominations have damaged the corporate man of God's new creation. Just as the corporate man created by God was divided and dispersed, and just as the children of Israel were divided and scattered, so the church as the new man has been divided. Although this division has been a frustration to the accomplishment of God's purpose, God cannot be defeated. His purpose will be fulfilled.

THE ONENESS OF GOD IN THE NEW JERUSALEM

Ultimately, God's purpose will be fulfilled through the new city, New Jerusalem. In the eyes of God, this new city has already come into existence. The principle with the new city is the same as that with the creation of man. After man was created by God, he was placed in front of a unique tree, the tree of life. He was also warned not to partake of the tree of the knowledge of good and evil. To eat of the tree of life is to keep the oneness, but to eat of the tree of the knowledge of good and evil is to fall into division, for it is to become involved with death, darkness, and the devil. Therefore, God's principle in His creation was to create one man and place him in front of a unique tree. This principle applies also to the New Jerusalem. In this unique city we see one throne, one street, one river, and one tree of life on either side of the river.

According to Ephesians 1:10, Christ, who is the center of God's economy, will ultimately head up all things through the church. Ephesians 1:10 will be fulfilled at the time of the New Jerusalem in the new heaven and new earth. The city of New Jerusalem will be used by God to head up all things in oneness. This means that for eternity there will be no division, only oneness.

ON THE GROUND OF ONENESS

From the beginning in Genesis 1 to the consummation in Revelation 22, we consistently see the divine oneness. God is one, and the man created by God was also one. This unique man was placed in front of the unique tree of life. After the corporate man created by God had been divided into nations, God selected one man, Abraham. Then, centuries later, He produced one church. Ultimately, God will have one eternal city with one throne, one street, one river, and one tree. In each of the four great acts of God, therefore, we see the principle of oneness. This should cause us to realize that the church today must be in oneness and must be built on the ground of oneness. Oneness is the very ground of the church. May the Lord grant us more light concerning this precious oneness.

CHAPTER TWO

LIFE AND LIGHT—THE ESSENCE OF ONENESS

Scripture Reading: Gen. 2:8-9; Lev. 1:1-2a; Psa. 36:8-9a; 133:1-3; Isa. 2:3, 5; John 17:11, 17, 21-23; Eph. 4:3-6; Rev. 21:22-24; 22:1-2; Eph. 1:10

In the previous chapter we pointed out that God's four great acts in the universe are related to creation, selection, the new creation, and the New Jerusalem in the new heaven and new earth. In each of these acts we see the matter of oneness. In God's creation there was one corporate man, and in God's selection of Abraham there was also just one man. Furthermore, the church, the one new man, is uniquely one as God's new creation. Finally, the new city in the new universe will be characterized by oneness. Actually, that city will be a corporate man. Hence, oneness is the basic element of God's acts.

A COMPREHENSIVE ONENESS

The reason for this oneness is that God Himself is one. Oneness is His nature. In all God's acts we see one origin, one element, and one essence. In God's creation we see one God and one corporate man. In His selection we also have the one God and one man. Moreover, in the church we have the one Spirit and one new man. Eventually, in the New Jerusalem we have the unique Triune God in the one city characterized by the one throne, the one street, the one river, and the one tree. Therefore, the oneness about which we are speaking is not a partial oneness; it is a great, complete, comprehensive oneness, a oneness in entirety. May we all be impressed with the vision of such a oneness. If we see the vision of the oneness of entirety, all the germs of division will be killed, and we will be delivered from every kind of division.

In this chapter we need to go on to see the essence of oneness. What is the essence of this great oneness, the oneness in entirety? The essence of this oneness is life and light.

ONENESS PRESERVED BY LIFE

Genesis 2:8 says, "Jehovah God planted a garden in Eden, in the east; and there He put the man whom He had formed." A garden is a place of life. After God created man, He put him in a place that was full of life. In the midst of this place, the garden in Eden, there was a tree called the tree of life. Not only was the garden a place of life, but at the center of this place there was the tree of life. The fact that the Creator put man in such an environment indicates that God was presenting Himself to man as the source of life and also as the supply of life.

Man, however, did not partake of the tree of life. Instead, he ate of the fruit of the tree of knowledge and, as a result, was eventually divided into nations. At Babel the man created by God for His purpose was divided into nations. This was the result of his having been seduced by Satan to eat of the tree of knowledge. Babel was the issue, the consequence, of the eating of the fruit of the tree of knowledge. This indicates that we should beware of anything that is not of life, for any such thing will result in division, Babel.

As we will see, there is a progression downward from Babel to Babylon and from Babylon to the great Babylon. Toward the beginning of the Old Testament, we have Babel, but toward the end, we have Babylon. Furthermore, toward the end of the New Testament, we have the great Babylon. Babel, Babylon, and the great Babylon all come from the source of the tree of knowledge. This means that the issue of partaking of the tree of knowledge is division.

Life, on the contrary, is the essence of oneness. The oneness in God's economy, the great oneness revealed in entirety in the Scriptures, can be preserved only by life. Without life, there can be no oneness.

Man's body illustrates this. Although there are many members in the body, all the members are one because they all share one life, the life of the body. Hence, the oneness of our physical body is its life. However, when a corpse is buried, it eventually decomposes because it does not have life. When life is removed from the physical body, the members of the body become detached. This illustrates the fact that the essence of the oneness of man's physical body is his physical life. If there is no life, there is no oneness.

In a very real sense, today's Christianity is not the Body; it is a corpse. The dry bones in Ezekiel 37 not only are an illustration of the situation of the children of Israel but may also be used as an illustration of the situation of Christians today. In this portion of the Word, the Lord caused Ezekiel to see a vision of a valley full of dry bones, bones that represent "the whole house of Israel" (v. 11). Originally, the children of Israel were a living body. But after they had been divided and scattered, they became dry bones, each detached from the others. Because the life had gone out of the bones, the essence of oneness was lost, and the bones were detached. In a negative way this reveals that life is the essence of oneness.

The one corporate man created by God was destined to produce a great number of descendants. How could these descendants remain one? By education? By some kind of power? By organization? The only way that oneness can be maintained is by life, in life, and with life. If Adam had eaten of the tree of life, all his descendants, even though they number in the millions, would have been kept in oneness. But because Adam partook of the tree of knowledge, the essence of division was injected into him, and his descendants were divided. The essence of Babel that is manifested in Genesis 11 was put into man in Genesis 3. This indicates that divisiveness and divisions are the issue of taking into our being something other than life. This element is the factor, source, and essence of division. The essence of oneness, on the contrary, is life. Only life can keep us in oneness.

GOD'S PRESENCE BEING LIFE TO ABRAHAM

Because of Babel, God was forced to give up the created race and to initiate another action—His selection of Abraham. The record in Genesis concerning Abraham does not use the words *life* or *light*. Nevertheless, in reality the matters of life and light have much to do with God's selection of Abraham. God's presence was with Abraham, and His presence was life to him. When Abraham was called by God, he did not know where to go. He did not have a map or any detailed directions. God's presence was his map, his guidance, and his supply. God's presence was life and everything to Abraham. Apart from God's presence, Abraham had nothing. He was surely a person who enjoyed the presence of God.

According to the record in the book of Genesis, God appeared to Abraham a number of times. Of course, when God appeared to him, He spoke to him. However, God's speaking was not as important to Abraham as God's appearing. Acts 7:2 indicates that Abraham was called by the appearing of the God of glory.

GOD'S SPEAKING
AND THE GROUND OF ONENESS

When Abraham's descendants, the children of Israel, made their exodus from Egypt and were brought into the wilderness, they built a tabernacle. God took up residence in this tabernacle, and as a result, it became the Tent of Meeting. The books of Leviticus and Numbers are filled with God's speaking. Leviticus 1:1 says that the Lord spoke to Moses out of the Tent of Meeting. Thus, the tabernacle, the Tent of Meeting, became the center of God's oracle, of God's speaking. Almost the entire book of Leviticus is a record of the Lord's speaking out of the Tent of Meeting.

If Moses and the children of Israel had departed from the Tent of Meeting, they could not have heard the word of God. Perhaps some of the children of Israel said, "God is everywhere. What right do you have to claim that He speaks only out of the tabernacle? You are too narrow and too exclusive. God is great, and He is not limited to a tent. You cannot say that God speaks only in one place. You simply cannot limit the unlimited God to your little Tent of Meeting." Yes, God is great, and He is omnipresent. But according to the Old Testament, He was happy to reside in the tabernacle built for Him in the wilderness by His people. Although heaven is spacious, God is not satisfied to remain there. Furthermore, He did not speak to His people from heaven; He spoke to them out of the Tent of Meeting.

Perhaps you are wondering what this has to do with the ground of the church. What does God's speaking, you may ask, have to do with the church ground? God's speaking is intimately related to the ground of oneness. If we are on this ground, which is the proper ground, we will have God's speaking day by day. But if we do not have the speaking of God, then we probably do not have the ground of oneness.

According to the book of Leviticus, God spoke from the Holy of Holies. The book of Leviticus is the result of this kind of divine speaking. Hence, God spoke from oneness. When this oneness is lost, God's oracle is lost also.

God's speaking brings in light, and light issues in life. When we do not have God's speaking, we have death and darkness. Death and darkness damage the Body and cause the members to become detached. Today's Christianity is filled with death and darkness because the genuine oneness in life is lacking.

RECEIVING LIGHT FROM THE SPEAKING GOD

Many times Christians have asked where we get the light that is conveyed in our writings. Regarding this matter of light, we have no reason to boast in ourselves. We receive our light from the speaking God. In order to receive light, we need God's speaking on the proper ground of oneness. Today God is still speaking in the Tent of Meeting, that is, in the center of oneness and on the ground of oneness. The Tent of Meeting is the ground, the base, of oneness. It is in this place that God's word is spoken to enlighten us. Apart from God's speaking, we are in darkness. But when His word comes, we are in light. Where God's speaking is, there is always light.

Many of us can testify that before we came into the Lord's recovery, we were in darkness. But now we have the sense that everything is clear and transparent. This is light. As you listen to messages, you experience the Lord's shining. Whether in the meetings or at home, you realize that you are under the Lord's enlightenment. This enlightenment comes from God's speaking on the ground of oneness. Therefore, to those who inquire about the source of the light we have received, we can only say that we have light because we are on the ground of oneness.

SATURATED

The children of Israel not only enjoyed the oracle of God; they were also saturated with the fatness of God's house (Psa. 36:8). God's house refers to the temple, which was the continuation and enlargement of the Tent of Meeting. In Psalm 36:9 the psalmist goes on to say, "With You is the fountain of life; / In Your light we see light." This verse is also related to the temple. Only in the temple could God's people enjoy the fountain of life. Furthermore, it was in the temple that they could see light in God's light. This is a further indication that the essence of the oneness of God's children is life and light.

LIFE MAINTAINING THE ONENESS

This is confirmed by Psalm 133, which begins with, "Behold, how good and how pleasant it is / For brothers to dwell in unity!" The psalm concludes like this: "For there Jehovah commanded the blessing: / Life forever." As this psalm makes clear, the blessing of life is related to the oneness of God's people.

Psalm 133 also speaks of the ointment and the dew of Hermon. The ointment and the dew were not omnipresent. On the contrary, they were to be enjoyed only at a particular place. If an Israelite wanted to share in the Lord's commanded blessing, he had to be in the place of oneness. This means that, at least three times a year, he had to make a journey to Mount Zion. Suppose some from the tribe of Dan were to say, "Why must we all go to one place for the worship of God? This is too narrow, too sectarian, and too exclusive. God is everywhere. We can stay here in Dan and enjoy singing praises to God." Those from Dan could enjoy singing, but unless they went to Mount Zion, they could not enjoy the commanded blessing.

The principle applies today also. If we would be under the Lord's commanded blessing of life, we must be on the ground of oneness. Dissenting ones may claim to have the commanded blessing, but actually they do not have it. Those who think that they do are superstitious. God is neither narrow nor exclusive, but He is definite. He is definite regarding His principle and His economy. God will never act contrary to His definiteness. Verse 3 of Psalm 133 is very definite. Here the psalmist says that *there,* upon the oneness, the Lord commands the blessing, life forever. In the oneness of brothers dwelling together the oil flows, the dew descends, and God's people enjoy life. If we lose the oneness, we lose the experience of the fine oil, the dew, and the blessing of life. If we would remain in the oneness, we must remain in life, because life maintains the oneness. This was true with the children of Israel, and it is true with us today.

PRESERVED IN LIFE AND LIGHT

We have seen that life is related both to the corporate man of God's original creation and to Abraham and his descendants, the children of Israel. Now we will go on to consider how life and light are the essence of the oneness of the church as God's new creation. In John 17 the Lord dealt with the matter of oneness not by teaching His disciples about it but by praying regarding it. This prayer reveals that oneness can be preserved and realized only in life. In verse 11 the Lord prayed, "Holy Father, keep them in Your name, which You have given to Me, that they may be one even as We are." To be kept in the Father's name is to be kept by His life, because only those who are born of the Father and have the Father's life can participate in the Father's name. The Son has given the Father's life to those whom the Father has given Him (v. 2). Hence, the believers enjoy the divine life as the essence of their oneness. If we are kept in the Father's life, we will be preserved in the oneness.

In verse 17 the Lord went on to pray, "Sanctify them in the truth; Your word is truth." To be sanctified is to be separated unto God from the world. In a very real sense, to be sanctified is to be preserved. Here the Lord prayed to the Father to sanctify the believers in the truth, which is the Father's word. As the Father's name is a matter of life, so the Father's truth is a matter of light. Life and light are, therefore, the very essence of oneness.

John 17:22 says, "The glory which You have given Me I have given to them, that they may be one, even as We are one." This verse indicates that the Triune God with His glory keeps the oneness of the believers. We are not kept in oneness by teachings or doctrines. We are preserved in oneness by life and light. The Triune God Himself is the life, and His word with His speaking is the light. By this life and this light the oneness is maintained. This is the reason that Ephesians 4 relates the oneness of the church, the Body of Christ, to the Triune God, to the Spirit, the Lord, and God the Father.

In the meetings of the church we enjoy the presence of the Triune God. This is especially true at the Lord's table meeting and at the prayer meeting. Through the prayers uttered by the saints in the prayer meeting, I enjoy the sweetness of the Lord. I can testify that whenever I come to the prayer meeting, I enjoy the Lord's anointing. Many of us can testify that we did not have such an enjoyment before we came into the Lord's recovery. But as we taste the sweetness of the Lord in the church meetings, we receive the supply of life and experience the enlightenment of life. Oh, how I am supplied and enlightened in the church prayer meetings! The Triune God with His glory surely is present with us. In the Triune God—the Father, the Son, and the Spirit—with His glory we are kept in oneness. For this reason, after the prayer meetings we often sense a fresh love for the saints. We also have the consciousness of having experienced more building up.

THE CYCLE OF LIFE, LIGHT, AND ONENESS

It is crucial for us to see that the oneness among God's children is preserved by life and light. It is not maintained through doctrine, organization, or maneuvering. We thank the Lord that in His recovery we have light and life. First, we are enlightened through the Lord's speaking. Then we receive the supply of life. Eventually, however, the life brings in more light. Actually, we enjoy the cycle of light and life, and life and light. The more light we have, the more life we enjoy; the more life we enjoy, the more light we receive. Light, life, and oneness go together. The more light, the more life; the more life, the more oneness; and the more oneness, the more light. This cycle of light, life, and oneness preserves the oneness.

However, we lose the oneness whenever we are in darkness and death. Darkness brings in death, and death causes detachment. But when we repent and confess to the Lord, we are cleansed by the precious blood. The cleansing of the blood is always related to the shining of light (1 John 1:7). As we are cleansed by the blood under the shining of light, we once again experience life. According to our experience, we can testify that the life, light, and blood in 1 John 1 also function as a cycle that keeps us in the oneness. But when we are in darkness, we lose the oneness, for we lose the proper ground of the church. The result is death and detachment. Once again we see that the essence of the oneness is life and light. The oneness is in life, with light, and on the proper ground.

THE ONENESS OF THE NEW CITY

Life and light are also the essence of the oneness of the new city, the New Jerusalem. Revelation 21 and 22 speak of this new city. In chapter 21 we mainly see the matter of light, whereas in chapter 22 we primarily have the matter of life. Revelation 21:23 says, "The city has no need of the sun or of the moon that they should shine in it, for the glory of God illumined it, and its lamp is the Lamb." In the New Jerusalem there will be no need of natural light because the city will be enlightened by the glory of the Triune God. The city will be illumined by the shining of God Himself. Furthermore, as the next verse says, "The nations will walk by its light" (v. 24). This reminds us of Isaiah 2:5: "House of Jacob, come and let us walk in the light of Jehovah." Light preserves oneness and rules out disorder. The light in the New Jerusalem will control, rule, guide, and keep everything in order. Hence, it will preserve the oneness.

Revelation 22:1 and 2 say, "He showed me a river of water of life, bright as crystal, proceeding out of the throne of God and of the Lamb in the middle of its street. And on this side and on that side of the river was the tree of life." The river of water of life flows out of the throne of God and of the Lamb to supply the city. The water of life here is a symbol of God in Christ as the Spirit flowing Himself into His redeemed people to be their life and life supply. In Revelation 22:1 the water of life is a river proceeding out of the throne of God and of the Lamb to supply and saturate the entire New Jerusalem. In this way the city will be filled with the divine life to express God in His glory of life.

As verse 2 says, the tree of life grows "on this side and on that side of the river." The one tree of life growing on the two sides of the river signifies that the tree of life is a vine, spreading and proceeding along the flow of the water of life for God's people to receive and enjoy. For eternity God's redeemed people will enjoy Christ as the tree of life as their eternal portion (vv. 14, 19). As the tree of life, Christ is the life supply available along the flow of the Spirit as the water of life. Where the Spirit flows, there the life supply of Christ is found. By the water of life and by the tree of life, the new city will be richly supplied for eternity. Through this abundant supply of life the oneness of the New Jerusalem will be forever maintained. It will not be possible for there to be any division. The light will shine throughout the city, and the life will water and supply the city. This life and light will eliminate the possibility of division. Even the nations that surround the new city will be one. At that time, all things in heaven and on earth will be headed up in Christ (Eph. 1:10). This will be the ultimate, universal, and eternal oneness. As we have pointed out again and again, this oneness will be kept and preserved in life and with light.

All the churches in the Lord's recovery must be in life and under the shining of light. By the shining of the light and through the watering and supplying of the life, we are one. There is no need for us to make arrangements or to organize anything. The essence of our oneness is not organization—it is life and light. May we all be deeply impressed with the fact that oneness can be prevailing and can be preserved only by life and light.

CHAPTER THREE

BABEL, BABYLON, AND THE GREAT BABYLON— ISSUES OF DIVISION

Scripture Reading: Gen. 2:9b, 17; 11:4, 9; 1 Kings 12:26-30; 15:34; 2 Chron. 36:5-20; 1 Cor. 1:11-13a; Rev. 17:3-5

TWO LINES

In the Bible there are two lines: the line of life and the line of death. These two lines come from the two sources that exist in the universe. One of these sources is God, and the other is the devil, Satan. Furthermore, each of these lines will have a particular issue, result. The line of life begins with the tree of life and ends with the New Jerusalem. The line of death begins from the tree of the knowledge of good and evil and, passing through the great Babylon, ends with the lake of fire. Oneness is on the line of life, originates with God, and issues in the New Jerusalem. Division, on the contrary, is on the line of death, originates with Satan, and issues in the great Babylon and, ultimately, the lake of fire. If we would see the great truth of oneness in the Bible, we need to be clear about these two sources, lines, and results. Then we will know where oneness and division belong.

Many Christians are careless about division because they do not see the seriousness of these two lines. Never regard division as an insignificant matter. Division is extremely serious, a matter of life or death. To be in oneness is to be in life, but to be in division is to be in death. In the previous chapter we pointed out that the essence of oneness is life and light. In this chapter we will go on to see that the issue of division is first Babel, then Babylon, and eventually the great Babylon.

NO MORE DIVISION

God's four great acts are related to creation, selection, the new creation, and the New Jerusalem in the new heaven and new earth. Apart from God—the only proper source in the universe—there is another source, Satan, with another element and issue. By the time of the New Jerusalem, this source, element, and issue will all be cast into the lake of fire. Therefore, in the new heaven and new earth God will be the unique source, and only His element and issue will remain. For this reason, in the new universe there will be no division. There will be no more death, no more sorrow, no more crying, no more pain, and no more darkness. We can go on to say that in the new heaven and new earth there will be no more sin, worldliness, flesh, self, or Satan. There will be no negative things whatever. This means that there will be no more division.

Division is all-inclusive. It comprises such negative things as Satan, sin, worldliness, the flesh, the self, the old man, and evil temper. If we are enlightened concerning the nature of division, we will see that it includes every negative thing. Do not think that division stands by itself and that it is not related to such things as the flesh, the self, and worldliness. Division is not only related to all negative things; it includes all negative things.

Just as division is all-inclusive, so, in the same principle, oneness is all-inclusive. It includes God, Christ, and the Spirit. Ephesians 4:3-6 indicates this. In the oneness revealed in these verses, we have God the Father, Christ the Lord, and the Spirit as the Giver of life. This oneness includes such positive things as our regenerated spirit and our transformed and renewed mind. Everything positive is included in the proper oneness.

The New Jerusalem will be the ultimate consummation of oneness and of all the positive things included in it. But the lake of fire will be the ultimate reservoir of division and all the negative things included in it. We may say that the lake of fire will be the eternal dead sea containing every negative thing in the universe. The lake of fire will be the ultimate and universal trash container. The New Jerusalem, on the contrary, will be the ultimate consummation and expression of oneness. This city will be characterized by one throne, one river, one tree, and one street. In the street will flow the river of water of life, and on either side of the river there will be the tree of life. Hence, we may properly call the one street of the New Jerusalem the street of life. This unique street will make division impossible. Division with all the negative things related to it will be found only in the lake of fire.

THE SOURCE OF BABEL

The first issue of division was Babel. The source of Babel was the tree of knowledge. If Adam had not eaten of the fruit of the tree of knowledge, it would have been impossible for his descendants to build the tower and city of Babel. According to the record in Genesis 3, Adam partook of the fruit of the tree of the knowledge of good and evil. As he ate of this fruit, the tree of knowledge actually entered into him and subjectively became part of him. The record of Genesis 4 indicates this. In this chapter we see hatred, murder, polygamy, and the invention of weapons used for war. Genesis 6 reveals a worsening of the situation. Man had become flesh (v. 3), and "the wickedness of man was great in the earth" (v. 5). Furthermore, as verse 11 declares, "The earth was corrupt before God, and the earth was filled with violence." When God looked upon the earth, He beheld its corruption, "for all flesh had corrupted its way upon the earth" (v. 12). As we all know, God judged that corrupt generation with the flood. However, not even this judgment caused man's nature to be changed. According to Genesis 11, man even dared to fight against God. In Genesis 11:4 they said, "Let us build ourselves a city and a tower...and let us make a name for ourselves." In seeking to make a name for themselves, they rebelled against God. The issue of this rebellion was division and confusion. This was Babel, the first result of division. As a result of the rebellion at Babel, mankind was divided.

THE SIGNIFICANCE OF BABEL

The division at Babel involved idolatry. Some historians believe that inscribed on the bricks used to build the tower and city of Babel were the names of idols. Joshua 24:2 says,

"Thus says Jehovah the God of Israel, Your fathers dwelt across the River long ago, Terah the father of Abraham and the father of Nahor; and they served other gods." This verse indicates that before Abraham was called of God, he served other gods in the land of Chaldea. This means that he worshipped idols. Hence, the division of mankind at Babel involved idolatry.

We see from these chapters in Genesis that division includes such negative things as hatred, murder, polygamy, war, corruption, rebellion, and idolatry. The issue of this all-inclusive element of division was first Babel with its division and confusion. The significance of Babel, therefore, is division and confusion.

THE ONENESS OF GOD'S PEOPLE

Although it was necessary for God to give up the created race, He did not give up His eternal purpose with man. Instead, according to His mercy, He appeared to a member of the Adamic race, Abraham, and called him out of his environment. In this we see God's selection. As we pointed out, in His selection of Abraham God acted according to His nature of oneness. For this reason, He selected one man, not a multitude of men. God charged Abraham to leave his country and his kindred and to go to the land that He would give to Abraham and his descendants.

Eventually, under the Lord's blessing, Abraham's descendants, the children of Israel, numbered in the hundreds of thousands. After the children of Israel made their exodus from Egypt, they entered into the good land, the land God had promised to Abraham. According to the book of Deuteronomy, God commanded them not to exercise their own choice regarding the place of corporate worship (ch. 12). Rather, they were to humble themselves before the Lord and accept His choice. By honoring the Lord in the matter of the place for corporate worship and of accepting God's choice of the unique place, the children of Israel were preserved in the oneness. According to God's choice, the temple was built on Mount Zion, and three times a year God's people were to make their journey there. The Holy of Holies in the temple built on Mount Zion was the center of the oneness of God's people. This center was the place of God's oracle, and it preserved the oneness of God's chosen people.

DIVISION CAUSED BY SELFISHNESS AND AMBITION

One day, however, the nation was divided into two kingdoms, into the northern kingdom of Israel and the southern kingdom of Judah. Jeroboam became the king of the northern nation, and Rehoboam, the king of the southern nation. After this division was formed, idolatry came in. Jeroboam not only caused division; he also set up idols in Bethel and in Dan (1 Kings 12:29). Having made two calves of gold, Jeroboam said to the people, "It is too much for you to go up to Jerusalem. Behold your gods, O Israel, who brought you up out of the land of Egypt!" (v. 28). The source of these idols was Jeroboam's selfish ambition. Jeroboam set up another center of worship because he feared the loss of his kingdom. First Kings 12:26 and 27 say, "Jeroboam said in his heart, Now the kingdom will return to the house of David. If this people go up to make sacrifices in the house of Jehovah at Jerusalem, the heart of this people will return to their lord, to Rehoboam the king of Judah; and they will slay me and return to Rehoboam the king of Judah." To prevent this from happening and to preserve his kingdom, Jeroboam set up idols in a rival center of worship. This clearly indicates that the origin of these idols was his ambition.

We need to apply this principle to the situation among Christians today. The divisions in Christianity are caused by selfishness and ambition. Because certain ones are ambitious to have their own empire, they neglect God's choice. Their ambition is to have a kingdom to satisfy their own selfish desire. In the Old Testament God's choice was a unique place: Mount Zion in Jerusalem. In this place the temple with the Holy of Holies as the oracle was built. Nevertheless, Jeroboam, an ambitious, selfish, and self-seeking man, set up another center of worship. Some may defend his action by pointing out that he did not establish a center for worldly entertainment but a place for the worship of God. However, this worship center was actually a cover-up for Jeroboam's ambition. The same is true today. Because of their selfishness and ambition, many Christian leaders have set up centers of worship. Apparently, these centers are established for the worship of God. Actually, they are set up to fulfill a man's ambition to have an empire. Hence, in a very real sense, the founders of many Christian groups are today's Jeroboams. The centers of worship set up by these present-day Jeroboams are actually centers of ambition. For this reason, "idols" can be found in those places.

According to the principle in 1 Kings 12:26-30, in many Christian groups there are "idols" set up to attract people and to hold them. These "idols" keep people from God. Following the example of Aaron at Mount Sinai, Jeroboam made two golden calves and told the people that they were the God who brought them out of Egypt. We may wonder why the children of Israel could be so blind as to accept these idols as God. Because we view the situation from afar, we can see it clearly. However, if we had been there, we probably would have followed Jeroboam and would have been one with him.

We need to be clear about the situation in Christianity today. If we are under the shining of the heavenly light, we will realize that in so many Christian groups "idols" have been set up in place of God. These "idols" attract people into those groups and then keep them there.

THE DESIRE FOR THE HOUSE OF GOD

We have pointed out that the genuine speaking of God was in the Holy of Holies in the temple. Psalm 27:4 expresses the deep aspiration of God's people with respect to the house of God. This verse says, "One thing I have asked from Jehovah; / That do I seek: / To dwell in the house of Jehovah / All the days of my life, / To behold the beauty of Jehovah, / And to inquire in His temple." How the psalmist desired to remain in the house of God to behold the Lord!

A similar longing is conveyed in Psalm 84. In verse 2 the psalmist says, "My soul longs, indeed even faints, / For the courts of Jehovah." In verse 10 he goes on to say, "A day in Your courts is better than a thousand; / I would rather stand at the threshold of the house of my God / Than dwell in the tents of the wicked." Here we see that the aspiration for the house of God was so strong that the psalmist desired even to be in the courts of the Lord; he was happy simply to stand at the threshold of the house of God.

Psalms 36 and 23 also express a deep desire for the house of the Lord. In Psalm 36:8 the writer says that God's people "are saturated with the fatness of Your house." It is in the house of the Lord that they are made to drink of the river of God's pleasures. Furthermore, it is in the house that they enjoy the fountain of life and see light in the light of God (v. 9). Psalm 23 concludes with the words, "I will dwell in the house of Jehovah / For the length of my days" (v. 6). In Old Testament times the godly ones aspired to be in the temple where God's presence was.

Such an aspiration repels evil. Simply the desire to be in the presence of God in the house of the Lord repels divisiveness and all the negative things it includes. This desire causes us to be godly, holy, and, eventually, to be one with the children of God.

As the children of Israel were chanting Psalm 133 on the way up to Mount Zion, surely it would have been impossible for them to hate or despise one another. Psalm 133 is a psalm of oneness. This oneness includes all positive attributes and virtues. By keeping the oneness, we spontaneously enjoy all these attributes and virtues. Furthermore, we have God's presence.

ONENESS KEEPING US FROM EVIL

By remaining in the oneness, we have the blessing commanded by God, life forever. However, if any of the children of Israel became divisive and refused to go to the temple on Mount Zion, they would automatically lose all these positive things. By separating themselves from the oneness of God's people, they would spontaneously become filled with such negative things as pride, hatred, criticism, rumors, and lies. Pretending to still be in fellowship with God, some might establish another center of worship. But, as the case of Jeroboam makes clear, such a divisive action opens the way for idolatry and all manner of evil things to enter in.

According to the record in the Old Testament, the sin of

Jeroboam, the sin of division, opened the way for every kind of evil to come in. Eventually, the situation of God's people was so corrupt that God caused Nebuchadnezzar, king of Babylon, to burn the house of God, to break down the wall of Jerusalem, and to carry away the people to Babylon. Thus, the captivity in Babylon was a further issue of division. Oneness is represented by Jerusalem, but division is represented by Babylon with all its evil.

Before coming into the church life, many among us were rather loose and did things according to our preference. But we can testify that shortly after we came into the Lord's recovery, our conscience began to function in a proper way. Little by little we dealt with things and discontinued certain practices. However, I know of many cases of those who experienced the very opposite of this as a result of leaving the church life. Their conscience began to lose its function, and the negative and worldly things they had put off gradually returned. Many resumed their former indulgence in worldly entertainments. Gradually, worldly things, even sinful things, returned. This indicates that oneness keeps us from evil, whereas division opens the door to evil.

More than thirty-five years ago a young woman from a wealthy family came into one of the church meetings in Chefoo. She was the very expression of worldliness, with her hair arranged in the form of a tower. Later, she said that she purposely styled her hair in that way as a protest. As she continued coming to the church meetings, her appearance began to change. We said nothing in the meetings about worldliness. We spoke only about loving Christ and the church. No one attempted to regulate the behavior of this young woman. But through coming into contact with the church, her conscience began to function. Spontaneously, without any human direction, she changed her hairstyle and manner of dress.

RIGHT WITH THE TEMPLE

For the children of Israel, the temple was the center of oneness. Hence, it was extremely serious for any of God's people to be wrong with the temple. Those who were right with the temple and who thereby maintained the oneness enjoyed God's presence, the blessing of life, and every other positive thing. But those who were wrong with the temple through divisiveness opened the door for all manner of evil. The same is true among Christians today. Many talk about holiness, victory, and spirituality. However, if we would have these virtues, we need to be in the proper oneness.

Consider again the experience of the children of Israel. Holiness, victory, and spirituality were not the result of their effort. These virtues were theirs simply because they were right with the temple, with the Holy of Holies, and with the Ark. When they remained in the oneness by being right with the temple, there was no need for them to try to be holy, victorious, or spiritual. Spontaneously, as part of the blessing of being in the oneness, they had these virtues. The reason many Christians have no victory, holiness, or spirituality is that they are wrong with the church and with the Ark, Christ, in the Holy of Holies. If we would be holy, spiritual, and victorious, we must be right with Christ and the church. In other words, we must remain in the proper oneness. It is the oneness that gives us access to all positive virtues and attributes.

When I was on the mainland of China, Brother Nee was the target for attack and opposition. Many of those who attacked and opposed him claimed that he, the churches, and the elders were wrong. When I first heard of such attacks and opposition, I wondered about the situation. Perhaps Brother Nee, the elders, and the churches were wrong. Eventually, however, I learned that every opposer of Brother Nee or the churches or the elders was even more wrong. I noticed that everyone who attacked the Lord's recovery underwent a spiritual decline. I do not know a single case of one who opposed or attacked the church who has improved spiritually. On the contrary, they have damaged themselves, and their condition has gradually worsened.

The only thing that can preserve us spiritually is the oneness. If we remain in the oneness, all positive things are ours. But if we take the way of division, we will be visited by all manner of evil things: hatred, jealousy, despising, and perhaps even such things as idolatry and fornication. Sooner or later, the divisive ones are carried away to "Babylon" as captives.

BABYLON THE GREAT

Revelation 17 also indicates that evil is related to division. This chapter presents a vision of Babylon the Great. According to verse 5, Babylon the Great is called "THE MOTHER OF THE HARLOTS AND THE ABOMINATIONS OF THE EARTH." Verse 4 exposes the fact that although this woman has a pleasant appearance, evil is concealed within her: "The woman was clothed in purple and scarlet, and gilded with gold and precious stone and pearls, having in her hand a golden cup full of abominations and the unclean things of her fornication." Outwardly, Babylon the Great is clothed in purple and scarlet and is gilded with gold, precious stone, and pearls. Furthermore, she has a golden cup in her hand. But this cup is full of abominations and the unclean things of her fornication. This is a picture of Christendom today. Christendom may have the golden cup, but the contents of the cup are idolatry, fornication, and every kind of evil. This is the element, the composition, of division. The ultimate issue of division is Babylon the Great, which is unveiled in Revelation 17.

Today's Christianity is altogether in a state of division. This division has opened the way for idolatry and spiritual fornication. In many cases, it has even opened the way for literal idolatry and physical fornication. As we have pointed out again and again, this is the issue of division.

THE SERIOUSNESS OF DIVISION

When we turned to the way of the Lord's recovery and came into the church life, the negative things associated with division were spontaneously set aside. However, as we have pointed out, those who forsake the proper oneness automatically become subject to the very evil things that once were put away from them. This should cause us to see that division is an extremely serious matter. Nothing is more dreadful than division. Satan knows that even the thought of division is sufficient to undermine our Christian life. It is like a termite that eats away at the very structure of a house. Therefore, even the thought of division must be repudiated.

When we are in the oneness, we are in life, and we enjoy

every positive virtue and attribute. Furthermore, our spiritual condition gradually improves. However, simply by accepting a divisive thought, the way is opened for evil to enter in once again.

We should never think that the church ground is not a matter of life. The ground of the church is the very base of our experience of life. To remain in oneness is to remain in life. Apart from the ground of the church, it is vain to talk about holiness or spirituality. Such things are directly related to oneness. It is marvelous to stay in the oneness, but it is terrible to be involved in division. Many of today's Christians have lost the Lord's blessing and grace simply because of division. This must be a warning to us in the Lord's recovery. Let us not repeat the history of the divisiveness of Christianity. May we all look to the Lord that He may preserve us in His oneness. We need to loathe even the thought of divisiveness. Praise the Lord for the oneness! May the Lord keep us in His presence by keeping us in this oneness.

CHAPTER FOUR

THE UNIQUE PLACE OF GOD'S CHOICE FOR KEEPING THE ONENESS

Scripture Reading: Deut. 12:1-8, 11, 13-15, 17-18, 26-28; 14:23; 16:16

In the first three chapters we considered certain principles related to oneness. Beginning with this chapter we will devote our attention to a number of details. The first of these details is the unique place of God's choice for keeping the oneness. In Deuteronomy 12, 14, 15, and 16 the unique place of God's choice is mentioned at least sixteen times. For example, in Deuteronomy 12:5 Moses charged the people to go "to the place which Jehovah your God will choose." According to Deuteronomy 14:23, God's people were to eat the tithes before the Lord their God in the place where He would choose. The fact that this matter of the unique place is mentioned again and again reveals its crucial importance.

The book of Deuteronomy is concerned with the enjoyment of the riches of the good land, a land described as flowing with milk and honey. The words recorded in this book, the last book of Moses, were given at a time when the children of Israel had come to the border of the good land and were about to enter in and possess it. Because Moses was concerned about their enjoyment of the good land, he spent a great deal of time to instruct them regarding life in the land. The book of Deuteronomy, therefore, is a word spoken by an aged, loving father concerning the future enjoyment of the children.

DESTROYING THE HEATHEN PLACES OF WORSHIP

In Deuteronomy 12 the desire of God's heart with respect to the living of the children of Israel in the good land is made known. Verse 1 speaks of the statutes and ordinances that

God's people were to observe in the land. In the next verse
Moses presents the first of these statutes: "You shall completely
destroy all the places where the nations whom you will dispossess have served their gods." In verse 3 Moses goes on to say,
"And you shall tear down their altars and crush their pillars;
and their Asherahs you shall burn with fire, and the idols of
their gods you shall cut down; and you shall destroy their name
from that place." Before the children of Israel could have a full
enjoyment of the riches of the good land, they had to utterly
destroy the heathen places of worship. All the pagan worship
centers had to be utterly destroyed. Every place in which the
heathen peoples had worshipped idols was to be destroyed, no
matter whether such places were "on the high mountains and
on the hills and under every flourishing tree" (v. 2). God's
people were to tear down their altars, crush their pillars, burn
their Asherahs, and cut down the idols of their gods. Furthermore, they were to destroy the names of them from that place.
Three main things were to be dealt with: the places, the idols,
and the names. This reveals that the good land was to be thoroughly cleared of all the heathen centers of worship.

Deuteronomy 12:4 says, "You shall not do so to Jehovah
your God." This indicates that the children of Israel were not
to worship the Lord in the same way as the heathen worshipped their gods.

THE PLACE FOR GOD'S NAME

In verse 5 Moses utters a very important word: "But to the
place which Jehovah your God will choose out of all your
tribes to put His name, to His habitation, shall you seek, and
there shall you go." After all the places of pagan worship had
been destroyed, God's people were to go to the place chosen by
God. In that unique place God would put His name. God's
name denotes His person. For His name to be in a particular
place means that His person dwells in that place. This indicates that the unique place of God's choice was God's dwelling
place, God's habitation.

A TYPOLOGICAL SIGNIFICANCE

According to the basic principle of the divine revelation in the Scriptures, the record in the Old Testament consists of types, figures, and shadows of matters found in the New Testament. If Deuteronomy 12 consists only of statutes given to the children of Israel, then this chapter cannot be applied to our situation today. However, the statutes recorded in this chapter have a spiritual significance. If we grasp the spiritual significance of these statutes, we will see that this portion of the Word was written not only for the children of Israel but also for us today. The apostle Paul realized that the history of the children of Israel was meant to have a typological significance for believers in the New Testament age. In 1 Corinthians 10:6 he says, "Now these things occurred as examples to us." In 1 Corinthians 10:11 he goes on to say, "Now these things happened to them as an example." For this reason Paul could say in Romans 15:4, "The things that were written previously were written for our instruction."

One of the most important types in the Old Testament is that of the good land, which is a full and complete type of Christ. Furthermore, the enjoyment of the produce of the good land typifies our enjoyment of the unsearchable riches of Christ (Eph. 3:8). Before you came into the church life, you probably never heard about the enjoyment of Christ. This was my situation. I knew that Christ was the Son of God, the Savior, and the Redeemer, but I had never heard that He could also be my enjoyment.

According to typology, the children of Israel first enjoyed the passover lamb as a type of Christ. First Corinthians 5:7 indicates clearly that the passover is a type of Christ: "Our Passover, Christ, also has been sacrificed." After the children of Israel had made their exodus from Egypt, they enjoyed the manna as they wandered in the wilderness. According to 1 Corinthians 10:3 and 4, the manna also is a type of Christ. It typifies Christ as our spiritual food, our daily manna. Although some Christians realize that manna is a type of Christ, not many see that the good land is also a type of Christ. Joshua 5:12 says, "The manna ceased on that day, when they ate of the produce of the land; and there was no longer manna for the children of Israel, but they ate of the yield of the land of Canaan that year." This verse clearly indicates that the manna was replaced by the produce of the good land. If the lamb of the passover and the manna are types of Christ as enjoyment for God's people, surely the good land with its rich produce is likewise a type of Christ for our enjoyment. Many of us can testify that only after we came into the church life in the Lord's recovery did we hear that Christ is the good land for our enjoyment.

ONLY ONE NAME

Before coming into the church life, most of us worshipped in places typified by the mountains, hills, and flourishing trees (Deut. 12:2). These were places where pagans worshipped idols. Today idols can be found both in Catholicism and in the Protestant denominations. Some Christians may agree that there is idolatry in Catholicism, but they may insist that there are no idols to be found in the denominations. Remember the word of Moses in Deuteronomy 12:3 about destroying the names. Every denomination has a name other than the name of Christ. For example, the Lutheran denomination adopts the name of Luther. In principle, to have a name other than the name of Christ is to set up an idol. Those in the denominations may argue that such names are not idols but simply means used to designate them as groups of Christians. However, to use a name in this way can be compared to a married woman taking a name of a man other than her husband. Such a practice is deplorable! Idols are found virtually everywhere in today's Christianity, for in so many places there is a name other than the name of Christ. Often a chapel or another building used for religious purposes is erected in the name of a certain person. In principle, this is an idol. We should have only one name— the name of Jesus Christ.

According to the type in Deuteronomy 12:3, we must destroy all the places and all the names. Furthermore, every pagan practice that has been adopted by Christianity must be eliminated. There is no room for such things in the church. The book *The Two Babylons* proves that Catholicism has assimilated many elements of paganism. For example, Christmas and Easter both have a pagan origin. Aspects of paganism are found not only in Catholicism but even in many of the denominations.

Spiritually speaking, we must destroy all the places, images, and names. For this reason there can be no reconciliation between the Lord's recovery and the denominations with their high mountains, hills, and trees for the worship of idols. Furthermore, we ourselves must be careful not to have any mountains, hills, or trees. We should have only Christ and only the unique place chosen by God for keeping the oneness.

LEARNING TO FEAR GOD

If we see that we must destroy all other places and go to the unique place chosen by God, we can proceed to see a number of other points revealed in Deuteronomy 12. First, we must learn how to fear God by going only to the place of His choice. Deuteronomy 14:23 says, "You shall eat before Jehovah your God, in the place where He will choose to cause His name to dwell, the tithe of your grain, of your new wine, and of your fresh oil and the firstborn of your herd and flock, that you may learn to fear Jehovah your God always." To go to the place of God's choice is to fear God. But to have the freedom to make our own choice of a worship center is not to fear God. Rather, it is to satisfy our lust.

Before you came into the church life, you may have traveled from one denomination to another. You went from place to place to satisfy your own desires or taste. To do this is not to fear God in a proper way. If we fear Him, we will come to the unique place that He has chosen.

God does not allow us the freedom to choose the place of worship. In this matter we must fear Him and simply come to the place of His choice. If we exercise the right to make our own choice, we follow the way of the heathen, the way of the nations. According to Deuteronomy 12, the children of Israel were to destroy all the places where the pagans worshipped their idols. In principle, we must do the same thing when we come to the church life. The choice of the place of worship is altogether the Lord's; it is not a matter of our preference. If we act according to our preference, we indulge our lust, for we satisfy our own desire regarding the place of worship. To behave in this way is to be like a woman who becomes involved with a man other than her husband. This is fornication. Just as a woman is limited to one man in marriage, so we are limited to the one place of God's choice as far as the corporate worship of God is concerned. We all must learn to fear the Lord our God. With respect to Christian meetings, we must fear God and do only what is according to His choice. God commands us to destroy all other worship centers and to go only to the place chosen by Him.

DOING WHAT IS RIGHT IN THE EYES OF GOD

Deuteronomy 12:8 says, "You shall not do according to all that we do here today, each man doing all that is right in his own eyes." It is dreadful to do what is right in our eyes. The Lord charges us not to behave in this way. Nevertheless, Christians today often say that to them a certain thing is right or wrong. To live in this way is to do what is right in our own eyes. But we must do what is right in the eyes of God. According to Deuteronomy 12:13, the children of Israel were not to offer their burnt offerings in places that seemed good to them: "Be careful that you do not offer up your burnt offerings in every place that you see." They were forbidden to offer burnt offerings on the mountains, on the hills, or under the flourishing trees. They had no right to worship God in the place of their choice. Instead, they had to do what was right in the eyes of God. Likewise, if we fear God, we will not do what is right in our own eyes. On the contrary, we will do what is right and good in the eyes of God. We need to pray, "Lord, have mercy on us so that we may not do what is right in our own eyes. Lord, help us to do what is right in Your eyes." We must learn to forget what we feel about things and care for the Lord's desire and choice. To us certain things may seem right, but how does the Lord feel about them? According to our estimation, it may be right to worship in a certain place, but the Lord may regard that place as a center for the worship of idols.

NOT ABUSING GOD'S GRACE

There are a number of reasons that the Lord commands us not to do what is right in our own eyes but to go to the place of His choice. The first of these reasons is that we should not abuse God's grace. The children of Israel were required to separate unto the Lord the top tenth, the tithe, of the produce of the good land. Furthermore, they were to offer to Him the firstlings of their flocks and herds. They had no right to keep the first-born or the top tenth for themselves. They were not allowed to eat them at home. Deuteronomy 12:17 and 18 say, "You may not eat within your gates the tithe of your grain or of your new wine or of your fresh oil, nor the firstborn of your herd or of your flock, or any of your vows which you vow or of your free-will offerings or of the heave offering of your hand; but you shall eat them before Jehovah your God in the place which Jehovah your God will choose." These verses indicate that the Israelites also had to present the sacrifices for vows and free-will offerings in the place of God's choice. No doubt, God's people presented the best of their produce and flocks as vows or freewill offerings. The point here is that all these offerings— the tithe, the firstlings, the vows, and the freewill offerings— could be enjoyed only in the place God had chosen to put His name. In other words, the children of Israel were required to go to the place of God's habitation with the top portion of the rich produce of the good land. This indicates that they were not permitted to abuse the grace of God. They had no right to enjoy the top portion according to their taste or preference. Rather, they had to enjoy them according to God's regulations. They had no choice except to bring these offerings to the place God had chosen for His name and His habitation.

This principle still applies in the church life today. If we do not come to the meetings of the church, we cannot enjoy the top portion of Christ. Whenever we deliberately stay home from the meetings, we find that we are not able to enjoy the top portion of Christ. Although we can have some enjoyment of the Lord in pray-reading or in fellowship, we cannot enjoy those por-tions of Christ typified by the firstlings, the tithes, the vows, and the freewill offerings. There is a divine regulation that prohibits us from abusing God's grace. According to this regu-lation, we must go to the house of God, the church, to enjoy the top portion of Christ. We are required to go to the place God has chosen; we are not allowed to act according to our own choice or preference. By accepting God's choice, we are subdued and are kept from abusing His grace.

THE LORD'S MOST THOROUGH DEALING

When we go to the place of God's choice, we experience the Lord's most thorough dealing with us. We are forced to be one with our brothers in Christ. Sometimes we may not desire to see a certain brother. Although we may attend the meetings of the church, we may try our best to avoid him. If we seek to avoid the presence of a certain brother, we will not be able to enjoy the top portion of Christ. We need to be thoroughly subdued. We should pray, "Lord, have mercy on me so that I may be right with my brother. I want to have no problem with him and to enjoy being in his presence." This illustrates the fact that when we come to the place of God's choice, we are dealt with by Him to the uttermost.

Suppose one Israelite had a problem with another and as a result did everything possible to avoid him. However, three times a year all the Israelite males were required to go up to Jerusalem. Those who refused were to be cut off from the fellowship of God's people. Eventually, any problem between the Israelites had to be settled. Otherwise, there would have been no way for them to come together in oneness on Mount Zion to worship God. As they ascended Mount Zion, the Israelites had to chant the words of Psalm 133: "Behold, how good and how pleasant it is / For brothers to dwell in unity!" Therefore, the unique place of God's choice preserved the oneness of His people. As long as the children of Israel followed God's choice, they had no alternative except to be one.

The situation is altogether different among Christians today. If one believer is not happy with another, he can simply go to a different place of worship. Most Christians regard themselves as free to choose a place to satisfy their own appetites. For this reason, among most Christians there is no subduing. But if we do not abuse God's grace but are fully subdued by coming to the place of His choice, the oneness will be preserved. No matter what kind of disposition we may have, we need to be subdued by coming to the place of God's choice. Otherwise, we will be cut off from the fellowship of the people of God. If we are subdued in this way, we will be preserved in the proper oneness.

THE PLACE WHERE THE LORD HAS PUT HIS NAME

Now we come to the matter of how to discern the place of God's choice. The first principle is that the place chosen by God must not have any name other than the name of God and Christ. Any place that has a name other than the name of Christ is not the place chosen by God. In Deuteronomy 12 God charged the people to destroy all the places with all the names. No name was allowed to remain. However, the unique place of God's choice was the place where the Lord put His own name. Hence, the place to which we are to go is the unique place where the Lord has put His name. For this reason, as we meet together in the church, we meet only in the name of the Lord Jesus Christ. In Matthew 18 the Lord Jesus spoke of us being gathered together *into* His name. Whenever we come together, we must come into His name. We should not adopt such denominational names as Methodist, Episcopalian, Presbyterian, Lutheran, or Baptist. All those names must be destroyed.

GOD'S DWELLING PLACE

The second principle is that the unique place of God's choice must be God's habitation, God's dwelling place. Ephesians 2:22 helps us to understand the significance of this principle for us today. In this verse we are told that God's dwelling place is our spirit. This means that the very place of God's choice is our spirit. Therefore, we discern God's chosen place by the name and by the human spirit. Today God's habitation is in our spirit.

Suppose we neglect or ignore the spirit and live instead in the realm of the mind, emotion, and will. This will make it difficult for others to recognize that we are in the place of God's choice. The place God has chosen is the spirit. In the church life we should not be known or characterized by the expression of opinion but by the exercise of the spirit. To go to the place of God's habitation is to go to the spirit.

A PLACE OF ENJOYMENT

Third, the place God has chosen is a place of enjoyment. In Deuteronomy 12 the word *eat* is used a number of times.

Verse 7 indicates that in the place God has chosen we will "eat before Jehovah." In verse 18 we see that the tithe of the produce of the good land and the firstlings of the herd and of the flock were to be eaten before the Lord in the place of His choice. These references to eating point to enjoyment. Therefore, the place God has chosen is a place of enjoyment. If in a particular place we do not sense the enjoyment of the Lord, we should question whether or not it is the place God has chosen. Where do we find the riches of Christ typified by the produce of the good land? At the times of the yearly feasts, the riches of the good land were to be found at Mount Zion in Jerusalem. According to the principle, today we may discern the place of God's choice by the enjoyment of the riches of Christ. The place of God's choice is characterized by this enjoyment.

A PLACE OF REJOICING

Finally, the place God has chosen is a place of rejoicing. Deuteronomy 12:12 and 18 speak of rejoicing before the Lord. This rejoicing is related to the eating of the firstfruits and of the firstlings. To rejoice is not simply to be happy. It is possible to be happy silently, but in order to rejoice we must utter something or make a joyful noise. The house of God is a place of rejoicing. The place where His people gather together must be not only a place of joy but also of rejoicing.

In this portion of the Word we have four ways to discern a proper and genuine church. A genuine church is where there is the unique name, the name of Christ. Furthermore, it is a place where the human spirit is prevailing, where the riches of Christ are enjoyed, and where we rejoice before the Lord. When the riches of Christ become our enjoyment, we will spontaneously be filled with joy and rejoice. Therefore, in the church life we have the name of the Lord and the exercise of the spirit. We also enjoy the riches of Christ and rejoice in the Lord. This is the place of God's choice, the unique place He has chosen for keeping the oneness.

CHAPTER FIVE

ENJOYING CHRIST
WITH GOD
ON THE GROUND OF ONENESS

Scripture Reading: Deut. 12:5-7, 13-14, 17-18; 1 Tim. 3:15b-16a; Heb. 10:25; Psa. 23:6; 27:4; 36:8-9; 42:4; 43:3-4; 66:13, 15; 84:1-8, 10-12; 92:10, 13-14; 133:1-3

Deuteronomy 12 is a rich chapter. According to verses 2 and 3, the children of Israel were to destroy the worship centers, the idols and images, and the names. Idols are found not only in the centers of pagan worship; they are also found in Catholicism, in Protestantism, and in the independent Christian groups. If we are enlightened by this portion of the Word, spiritually speaking we will destroy all the places, idols, and names.

Often the pagan centers of worship were located on mountains or hills or under flourishing trees (v. 2). The mountains and hills signify the exaltation of something other than Christ, and the flourishing trees signify things that are beautiful and attractive. The various worship centers in today's Christianity lift up something other than Christ. In principle, these centers of worship are on a mountain or hill, the high places. However, God's people were to come to Mount Zion, the unique place chosen by God for corporate worship. The worship at the high places was a factor in the dispersion of the children of Israel.

In principle, we must destroy all the places, idols, and names. To do this is to do what is right in the eyes of the Lord. But if we insist on our own choice, we are doing what is right in our own eyes. We must fear the Lord and go to the place He has chosen.

THE WAY OF DIVISION

Christianity has followed the world by taking the way of division. From the time of Babel, the people of the world have been divisive. The reason for this divisiveness is that people insist on their own choice or preference. For this reason human society today is altogether divisive. The church should be different. As the unique place chosen by God, the church should have no division. This means that the church should not follow the customs of the nations or the pagan practices of human society. Nevertheless, from the time of the second century, the church has been divided over such things as opinions concerning the person of Christ. The different schools of Christology, the study of the Person of Christ, became "mountains" and "hills." Thus, the church was divided not mainly by evil things but mainly by good things, even by opinions about Christ.

As we all know, in the centuries following the Reformation, Christianity has had hundreds of divisions. After World War II the independent groups began to flourish in the United States. In 1963 I was told that in Southern California alone there were more than a thousand such groups. The history of Christianity proves that the most striking aspect in which it has followed the world is the matter of division. The pagan practice of division, of following our own choice, taste, or preference, is found throughout Christianity. Even to entertain the thought of division is to take the way of the pagan system, the divisive practice of the custom of the nations.

When the children of Israel entered the good land, pagan centers of worship could be found everywhere. In some places there were altars, in other places there were dedicated pillars or wooden symbols, and in still other places there were graven images of heathen gods. The land of Canaan was filled with idols. Therefore, God charged the children of Israel to destroy all these things and to come to the unique place chosen by God. In principle, we must do the same thing today.

Today many Christians look for a so-called church in the same way that people shop for a pair of shoes. They may go from one shoe store to another until they find something to match their preference. Some Christians spend years going from one place of worship to another, continually looking for a place that suits their taste or satisfies their desire. Such Christians are church travelers. Before I came into the church life, I also did a certain amount of this kind of traveling. But when I came into the church in the Lord's recovery, my traveling ended. I knew I had come to the place of God's choice.

Deuteronomy 12:5 says, "To the place which Jehovah your God will choose out of all your tribes to put His name, to His habitation, shall you seek, and there shall you go." When the children of Israel entered into the good land, they were not to follow the practice of the nations. They were not to choose places according to their own preference; rather, they were to go to the unique place chosen by God. As revealed in other books of the Old Testament, this unique place was Mount Zion in Jerusalem where the temple, the house of God, was built.

GOD'S CONCEPT OF WORSHIP

In the place God had chosen, the children of Israel were to eat before the Lord and rejoice (v. 7). Nowhere in the book of Deuteronomy were God's people told that they should go to the unique place to engage in mere "worship." Of course, they were expected to worship the Lord in the place He had chosen but not to worship according to their concept of what worship is. Instead, they were to worship according to God's thought, concept, of worship. According to the natural, human concept, to worship is to kneel, to bow down, or to prostrate ourselves before God. Even Muslims worship in such a way in their mosques. Once I visited a Muslim mosque at the time of worship. I noticed that among the worshippers there was no sense of enjoyment. On the contrary, due to the lack of enjoyment, many of those worshippers looked older than their years. The worship indicated in Deuteronomy 12 is not a matter of kneeling, bowing, or prostrating ourselves. According to this chapter, to worship is to eat before the Lord. When they came to the place God had chosen, God's people were to eat the top portion of the offerings and sacrifices before God.

Deuteronomy 12:6 describes this: "There you shall bring your burnt offerings and your sacrifices and your tithes and the heave offering of your hand and your vows and your freewill offerings and the firstborn of your herd and of your flock." The best portion of the produce of the good land was to be eaten before the Lord in the place He had chosen. The children of Israel were required to set aside the tithe, the top tenth, of the produce of the land and bring it to the place of God's choice. Moreover, they were to set aside the firstlings of their herds and flocks. Three times a year—at the Feast of Unleavened Bread, the Feast of Weeks, and the Feast of Tabernacles—they brought the tithes and the produce to the house of God in Jerusalem. During these feasts they could enjoy all these riches in the presence of the Lord. They were forbidden, however, to enjoy these particular portions at home. They could enjoy them only at the times of the feasts and only in the place designated by God. Their eating of the offerings was their worship of God. After bringing the tithes and sacrifices to the proper place, they offered them on the altar. Then they ate of the very things they had offered. There was a portion for God, a portion for the priests, and a portion for the one who presented the offering. Therefore, God's people enjoyed the rich produce of the good land before God and with God. This was the genuine worship of God.

Have you ever thought that this is the kind of worship God desires? In Deuteronomy 12 there is no mention of singing or even of praying. According to this portion of the Word, proper worship is a matter of eating before God the rich produce of the good land. The good land is a type of Christ, and the rich produce of the land is a type of the riches of Christ. Hence, the worship God desires from us is that we eat and enjoy the riches of Christ in His presence. Spiritually speaking, we all need to gain more weight by eating more of Christ. The focal point of Exodus, Leviticus, Numbers, and Deuteronomy is the eating of Christ. If we do not eat of Christ, we cannot worship God. The worship God is seeking is related to the enjoyment of Christ. The various offerings and sacrifices in Deuteronomy 12:6 all typify aspects of Christ for our enjoyment. May we all be impressed with the fact that proper worship is a matter of eating the produce of the good land, that is, of enjoying with God and before God the riches of Christ in the unique place chosen by God.

Throughout the history of Christianity, this kind of worship has been lost. But I have the full assurance that the Lord is in the process of recovering it. In the church He is bringing us back to genuine worship, back to the enjoyment of Christ in the unique place of God's choice. Before God and with God, we enjoy Christ on the ground of oneness. Praise Him for the eating, the enjoyment, of the riches of Christ!

EATING AND REJOICING

Deuteronomy 12:7 also says, "You and your households shall rejoice in all your undertakings, in which Jehovah your God has blessed you." This indicates that the children of Israel not only ate before the Lord; they also rejoiced before Him. Eating and rejoicing go together. As the children of Israel enjoyed the produce of the good land in the presence of God, they rejoiced. Apart from the riches of the land of Canaan, they had nothing to eat and therefore no reason to rejoice. Both the eating and the rejoicing were dependent upon the riches. Often when we are invited to a dinner or to a feast, we rejoice when the food is set on the table. In the same principle, the riches of Christ are the factor, the cause, of our rejoicing in the place of God's choice.

FOUR CHARACTERISTICS
OF THE PROPER CHURCH LIFE

In the foregoing chapter we pointed out four characteristics of the proper church life: the name, the habitation, the enjoyment, and the rejoicing. The fact that the church is God's habitation, God's dwelling place, indicates that His presence is in the church. God does not simply visit the church or dwell there temporarily, as if it were a motel. As the house of the living God, the church is God's home, God's habitation. Therefore, God's presence is in the church. In the church we enjoy the riches of Christ and we rejoice in the Lord. This is the proper, genuine, and normal church life. Here we have the Lord's name and presence. We come to the church to meet Him, to see Him, and to enjoy His presence. Here we enjoy the riches of Christ with God. As we enjoy these riches, we rejoice in the Lord.

Many of us can testify that in other places we did not have the reality or actuality of the Lord's name and presence.

Furthermore, we did not have the enjoyment of the riches of Christ or the rejoicing. For the most part, these four characteristics cannot be found in today's centers of Christian worship. Outwardly, the name of Christ may be there; but in reality the Lord's name is not to be found there. Furthermore, the presence of the Lord is not in such places. A. W. Tozer makes this point emphatically in an article entitled "The Waning Authority of Christ in the Churches." According to our experience, we can also testify that in the various Christian centers of worship there is no enjoyment of Christ and no rejoicing that comes from this enjoyment. However, in the place chosen by God, the church, we have the Lord's name, His presence, the enjoyment of the riches of Christ, and the rejoicing in the Lord.

DWELLING IN THE HOUSE OF THE LORD

In the Psalms we see how the Old Testament saints enjoyed the Lord in the unique place of God's choice. Let us now consider a number of verses that testify of this enjoyment. In these verses we see how God's people worshipped Him through enjoying the riches of the good land in God's presence. The ancient saints surely enjoyed Christ with God in the unique place of God's choice. The verses we will consider are the outstanding verses in the Psalms related to the enjoyment of the riches of the good land in the place of God's choosing.

Psalm 23:6 concludes with the words, "I will dwell in the house of Jehovah / For the length of my days." Christians love Psalm 23 mainly because it speaks of the Lord as the Shepherd. However, the ultimate goal of the Lord's shepherding of us is the house of the Lord. According to this psalm, the Lord leads us from one station to another until we are brought to the house of the Lord. He makes us to lie down in green pastures, He leads us beside waters of rest, He guides us on the paths of righteousness, He takes us through the valley of the shadow of death, and then He brings us to the battlefield. Ultimately, however, He causes us to dwell in the house of the Lord. It is in the Lord's house that goodness and lovingkindness are with us all the days of our life. We should not simply visit in the house of the Lord; we should dwell there for the length of our days, that is, forevermore.

In verse 6 there is a parallel construction. On the one hand, goodness and lovingkindness will follow us all the days of our life. On the other hand, we will dwell in the house of the Lord for the length of our days. There is, therefore, a parallel between *the days of my life* and *the length of my days*. This indicates that goodness and lovingkindness will be with us as we dwell in the house of the Lord. If we desire to share in the Lord's goodness and lovingkindness, we need to be in the house of the Lord. Today the house of the Lord is the church. Outside the church we cannot have the full enjoyment of the Lord's goodness and lovingkindness. But in the church we enjoy the goodness and lovingkindness of the Lord for the length of our days.

ONE DESIRE

Psalm 27:4 says, "One thing I have asked from Jehovah; / That do I seek: / To dwell in the house of Jehovah / All the days of my life, / To behold the beauty of Jehovah, / And to inquire in His temple." Here we see that the one desire of the psalmist was to dwell in the house of the Lord all the days of his life. The house of the Lord for us today is the church. If we are like the psalmist, we shall desire to dwell in the church all the days of our life. Here in the church we behold the beauty of the Lord. This refers to the Lord's presence. Furthermore, we inquire in His temple. We do not pray according to our will, but we inquire concerning His will, seeking His desire. If we would behold the beauty of the Lord and inquire in His temple, we need to dwell in the Lord's house, the church.

ENJOYING CHRIST'S RICHES

Psalm 36:8 says, "They are saturated with the fatness of Your house, / And You cause them to drink of the river of Your pleasures." In typology the fatness of the Lord's house refers to the rich produce of the good land. All the riches that were offered to God in the house became the fatness of the Lord's house. The fulfillment of this type is in Christ; He is the reality of the fatness of the Lord's house. In Old Testament times God's people could enjoy this fatness only in the place God had chosen for His habitation. For this reason the psalmist declares that God's people will be saturated with the fatness of His house.

This verse also says, "You cause them to drink of the river of Your pleasures." As we enjoy the fatness in the house of God, we drink of the river of the Lord's pleasures. These pleasures are a river of joy to those who come to the place of God's choice. Such pleasures come from the enjoyment of the fatness in the house of God. Hence, in the Lord's house we are full of joy as we drink of the river of God's pleasures.

Verse 9 goes on to say, "With You is the fountain of life; / In Your light we see light." In these verses we have the fatness, the pleasures, the life, and the light. We enjoy not only the river but also the fountain. This rich enjoyment is ours in the house of God, the church. In the church we are saturated with the riches of Christ, and we are full of pleasure and joy. There is even a river of pleasures of which we may drink. Furthermore, we have the fountain of life. This life becomes the light in which we see light.

Our experience of all these aspects of Christ's riches becomes the genuine worship we render to God. This worship is the basic element of the church life. The church life consists of worship that comes from the enjoyment of Christ. This enjoyment fills us with joy and pleasure, pleasure that even becomes a river of which we drink. Eventually, we come to the fountain of life, and in the Lord's light we see light. Here there is no darkness, death, weakness, or emptiness. On the contrary, we are satisfied and joyful as we drink of the Lord's pleasures and enjoy life and light. The worship produced by this enjoyment is the worship God desires today. This enjoyment and this worship constitute the proper, normal church life. Although the Christian religion knows nothing of such worship, the Lord is recovering it in the church life today.

GOING WITH THE MULTITUDE
TO THE HOUSE OF GOD

In Psalm 42:4 the psalmist declares, "These things I remember, / And I pour out my soul within me: / That I passed through with the throng; / I led them to the house of God / With the voice of a joyous shout and praise, / The festal multitude."

Here the psalmist recalls the enjoyment of going with the multitude to the house of God. He remembered how they went to God's house with a voice of a joyous shout and praise. With the multitude he kept the days of feasting. When the psalmist uttered these words, he was in captivity, having lost the enjoyment related to the Lord's house. But as he remembered this enjoyment, he poured out his soul within him.

This verse is a window through which we can see how the saints enjoyed the produce of the good land in the house of God. They went to the Lord's house with joy and praise, entering joyfully into the presence of God. There in the Lord's presence they enjoyed the top portion of the produce of the land. In principle, this is our experience in the church life today. We come together with a multitude to enjoy Christ by keeping the feast. Every time we come to the meetings of the church, we feast on the riches of Christ. Here in the Lord's house we truly enjoy Christ with God.

LIGHT AND TRUTH

Psalm 43:3 says, "Send forth Your light and Your truth; / They will lead me; / They will bring me to Your holy mountain / And to Your tabernacles." Light and truth are not two separate things; they are two aspects of one thing. As we have pointed out elsewhere, in the Gospel of John we have grace and truth, but in the first Epistle of John we have love and light. Truth is the shining of light. When the light shines upon us, we receive the truth, the reality. However, as we go to God in fellowship, we are in the light. Thus, on our end there is truth, but on God's end there is light. According to Psalm 43:3, we need both light and truth.

This verse indicates that light and truth lead us and bring us to the Lord's holy mountain and to His tabernacles, that is, to the house of God. Day by day we are led by the light and the truth that come from the house of God. In 1 Timothy 3:15 and 16 we see that the church, the house of the living God, is the pillar and base of the truth. This indicates that truth is to be found in the church, the house of God. When we have truth, we also have light. Hence, both light and truth are in the church.

As this verse makes clear, light and truth have a specific

and definite function: to bring us to the holy mountain and to God's tabernacles, that is, to lead us to the place of God's choice and to His habitation. Today many Christians are seeking light and truth, but not many seek them for the purpose of being led to God's chosen place. However, if our purpose is to be brought to the holy mountain and to God's dwelling place, light and truth will surely come to us. Many of us can testify that before we came into the church life, we received light and truth simply because we had begun to consider the church. Because we had the thought of coming to the church, light and truth came to us. But when we were hesitant regarding the church, the light and truth seemed to disappear for a period of time. However, when we realized that we must take the way of the church, light began to shine again, and truth appeared more fully than before. Then when we came into the church life, we were in the daylight and received much truth. This testifies that light and truth have led us to God's holy mountain and have brought us to God's dwelling place, the church.

PRESENTING OUR OFFERINGS TO THE LORD

Let us go on to Psalm 66. Verse 13 says, "I will come into Your house with burnt offerings; / I will pay my vows to You." In verse 15 the psalmist goes on to say, "I will offer to You burnt offerings of fatlings / With the smoke of rams; / I will offer cattle with goats." The psalmist realized that only in God's house, the temple, could he offer burnt offerings and sacrifices. He knew that only by going to the place of God's choice could he offer sacrifice to God. According to the type, we today must also go to the place of God's choice, the church, if we would present our offerings to the Lord. The children of Israel were required to go to the temple in order to present their offerings to God. God did not accept offerings in any other place. If an Israelite living in Dan had expressed the desire to offer something to God in Dan, the Lord would have said, "I cannot accept an offering presented to Me there. I accept offerings only at Mount Zion." God was not narrow, but He had chosen to make the temple the focal point of His attention. He had chosen Mount Zion as the unique place of worship. Only in that place could His people present their offerings to Him.

This principle applies in the church life today. Many of us can testify that when we attempted to offer something to God outside the church, that offering was not very pleasant. I dare not say that Christians cannot offer anything to God outside the church. But I can testify that to do this apart from the church life is not altogether pleasant. According to the type, our offerings should be presented at the unique place of God's choice.

SUBDUED BY COMING TO GOD'S CHOSEN PLACE

We may think that this requirement is ridiculous. God's thought, however, is higher than ours. By being limited to God's chosen place, we are kept from abusing God's grace, and we are subdued with respect to our desires, temperament, and disposition. We all have our particular natural disposition, temperament, and characteristics. But no matter what our peculiarities may be, we all must be subdued. If we remain in our natural life and in our natural disposition with its particular characteristics, it will be impossible for us to have the kind of worship God is seeking. We all must be subdued by coming to the unique place, to the unique ground. This means that we all need to be subdued by the church. If we are not willing to be subdued, we will fight with the elders, with the other brothers and sisters, and even with our husband or wife. Even concerning spiritual things, the things of God, we will have disagreements with others. We may prefer matters to be a certain way, but someone else may prefer another way. How we all must be subdued by taking the way of the church!

In the *Life-study of Colossians* we pointed out that the peace of Christ must arbitrate in our hearts. However, apart from the church life, it is difficult to experience the arbitrating peace of Christ. Yes, the peace of Christ does arbitrate within our hearts, but it does so in the context of the church life. In a very real sense, it is the church that is the arbitrator. The way of the church is the way of being subdued. Because we are subdued by the ground of the church, we are preserved in oneness. The unique place of God's choice keeps us from abusing God's grace, and it also subdues us. Furthermore, this unique way gives us the real enjoyment of Christ. When we have the genuine enjoyment of Christ, we are one. We are one in the enjoyment of Christ, that is, in the eating of the rich produce of the good land. But as we have pointed out, we can present our offerings of this produce only in the place of God's choice. Like the psalmist, we must bring our offerings to the house of God.

INCENSE TO GOD

Psalm 66:15 says, "I will offer to You burnt offerings of fatlings / With the smoke of rams; / I will offer cattle with goats." I am fond of the phrase *with the smoke of rams*. The Chinese translation speaks of the fragrant offering of rams. When our offering becomes an incense to God, it means that there is fragrance in our offering. When we bring our burnt offerings to the church and offer them to the Lord in the church, there is incense to match our offerings. This incense is fragrant and pleasant to the Lord.

It is possible to present offerings to the Lord outside the church, but with these offerings there is no fragrance. However, when we offer something to the Lord in the church, we sense that we present our offerings "with the smoke of rams." Oh, the fragrance of the offerings presented to God in the church! Although this fragrance is especially for God, we can sense it also. We cannot experience such incense apart from the church life. Only in the church life can the offerings be presented to God in a proper way, in a way that is fragrant and satisfying to Him.

THE LOVELINESS
OF GOD'S TABERNACLES

Psalm 84 is exceedingly rich. Verses 1 and 2 say, "How lovely are Your tabernacles, / O Jehovah of hosts! / My soul longs, indeed even faints, / For the courts of Jehovah; / My heart and my flesh cry out / To the living God." Verse 1 speaks not only of one tabernacle but of many tabernacles. No doubt these tabernacles signify the local churches. The local churches can be so lovely to us that we are even homesick for them. According to verse 2, the psalmist longs even for the courts of the Lord. In his estimation, not only the inside of God's dwelling is lovely; the courts also are lovely. The reason God's tabernacles are lovely is that the living God is there. God's presence in the local churches makes the churches lovely and lovable.

Verse 3 says, "At Your two altars even the sparrow has found a home; / And the swallow, a nest for herself, / Where she may lay her young, / O Jehovah of hosts, my King and my God." No doubt, we are the sparrows and the swallows, little creatures who are small and frail. Yet the sparrows have found a home, and the swallows have found a nest where they may lay their young. How sweet is the feeling of the psalmist concerning the house of God! It is a place for little sparrows to abide, a place for the swallow to build a nest for herself, where she may lay her young. In the house of God, we, the sparrows and the swallows, find a home at the Lord's altars. At the Lord's altars we find a nest, a place of nourishing and cherishing and a place of rest.

In ancient times, both in the tabernacle and in the temple, there were two altars: one in the outer court and the other in the Holy Place. The altar in the outer court, the bronze altar, was the place for the offerings that dealt with the negative things, cleansed the Lord's people, and delivered them from all problems. The altar in the Holy Place, the golden altar, was the altar of incense, which signifies the resurrected Christ as our acceptance to God. Hence, these altars signify Christ in crucifixion and in resurrection. It is here that we find our home and our rest in the house of God.

All the little ones, the sparrows and swallows, in the local churches must realize and apprehend the significance of the crucifixion and resurrection of Christ, with all that He has accomplished and attained for us. We need to apprehend how Christ is the crucified One at the offering altar and the resurrected One at the incense altar. Through such an apprehension, we will enjoy the goodness of the crucified and resurrected Christ. At these altars we find a true resting place, a nest where we are nourished and cherished and where we may be at rest. How marvelous is this enjoyment in God's dwelling place, the local churches!

In verse 4 the psalmist goes on to say, "Blessed are those who dwell in Your house; / They will be praising You all the day long" (Heb.). We should not simply visit the house of God; we should dwell there all the day long. According to this verse, those who dwell in the Lord's house are blessed. They even praise the Lord all day long. Whenever we meet together, we should spend much time in praising. Praising should occupy more time in the meetings than teaching. May we all learn to praise the Lord.

In verse 5 the psalmist continues, "Blessed is the man whose strength is in You, / In whose heart are the highways to Zion." In the church we have our strength in God, and our heart is filled with the highways to Zion. If we would experience this, we must be in the house of God.

Verse 6 says, "Passing through the valley of Baca, / They make it a spring; / Indeed the early rain covers it with blessings." *Baca* means "weeping." In the church life we may pass through the valley of weeping, but we can cause this valley to become a place of springs. Furthermore, instead of tears, rain comes to fill the pools. Such an experience is to be found only in the house of God.

Furthermore, in the church life we go from strength to strength and appear before God (v. 7). In the church we realize that "a day in Your courts is better than a thousand." Those who enjoy the church life can say, "I would rather stand at the threshold of the house of my God / Than dwell in the tents of the wicked" (v. 10).

Verse 11 indicates that the church life is the place of fullest blessing: "Jehovah God is a sun and a shield; / Jehovah gives grace and glory; / He does not withhold anything good / From those who walk uprightly." Here in the house of God we enjoy God as a sun and a shield. The sun is for supply, and the shield is for protection. Here in the church life the Lord is our supply and safeguard. Furthermore, here we enjoy His grace and His glory. Grace is the inner enjoyment, whereas glory is the outward expression. In the church life we have the inner enjoyment of grace and the outward expression of glory. Oh how blessed is the church life!

Psalm 84 concludes with the words, "O Jehovah of hosts, blessed is the man / Who trusts in You" (v. 12). We may trust in God outside the local church, but it is rather difficult. We can testify, however, that it is very easy to trust in God in the church. The house of God is the proper place for us to exercise our trust in the Lord.

EXALTED, MINGLED, PLANTED, AND FLOURISHING

In Psalm 92 we see even more aspects of the enjoyment in the house of God. Verse 10 says, "You have exalted my horn like that of a wild ox; / I am anointed with fresh oil." In the church life we can be as strong as a wild ox. Furthermore, we have two horns that are exalted. This is possible only in the house of God. Moreover, in God's house we are anointed, even mingled, with fresh oil. Outwardly we have two exalted horns, and inwardly we are mingled with fresh oil. Everyone in the church life can have horns like a wild ox and be mingled with fresh oil.

Many who have come into the church life have experienced their horn being exalted. Before we came to dwell in the church, we were low and frequently defeated. But when we came into God's dwelling place, we sensed that our horn was exalted over our enemy. Furthermore, we sensed that we were mingled with fresh oil. In God's house we daily have the sense of being mingled with fresh oil. Day by day we sense something very fresh—this is the oil that is being mingled with us. The reason we are fresh is that we are mingled with fresh oil.

Verse 13 says, "Planted in the house of Jehovah, / They will flourish in the courts of our God." We should not simply dwell in the Lord's house; we should also be planted there. Have you been planted in the church life? Those who leave the church have not been planted in the church. Once you have been planted in the house of the Lord, you cannot leave it.

If we have been planted in the house of the Lord, we will flourish in the courts of God. This is a very meaningful expression. We are in both the house and the courts. Our root is set in the house, but our branches reach out into the courts. The flourishing is not mainly with the root; it is with the branches.

Verse 14 continues, "They will still bring forth fruit in old age; / They will be full of sap and green." Although I am an elderly person, I am more fruitful today than I was years ago. As this verse says, I am still bringing forth fruit in old age, and I am full of sap and green. We may flourish to such an extent that even when we are old we bring forth fruit. This is possible only in the church as the house of God. If we are planted in the divine habitation, we will flourish in the courts of our God, bring forth fruit even in old age, and be full of sap and green. The longer we dwell here, the younger we become. This is the result of dwelling in the house of the Lord.

These verses from Psalm 92 indicate that the unique place of God's choice is not only the proper place to offer sacrifice and to worship God; it also is the proper place for the growth in life. The proper Christian life is a life that is planted in the church and that flourishes in the courts of the church life. Here in the church life we have the genuine growth in life. As we grow, we are filled with sap and green. As a result, spontaneously we are holy, spiritual, and victorious.

Who is more holy, spiritual, and victorious than those who are planted in the house of God? No one can surpass them in these respects. Those who dwell in the Lord's house have no need to seek holiness, spirituality, or victory. These attributes spontaneously become theirs because they are planted in the church life and are flourishing in the church life. Because they are full of sap and green, they are automatically holy, spiritual, and victorious. This indicates that the proper way for us to have the Christian life is to be in the normal church life. Apart from the proper church life we cannot be holy, spiritual, or victorious. These attributes are found in the church life. When we are planted in the church life, we will flourish with holiness, spirituality, and victory. As a result, we will worship God not merely in an objective way but with a subjective, dispensational worship that comes out of the enjoyment of Christ in the presence of God.

DWELLING IN UNITY

The last psalm we will consider here is Psalm 133. Verse 1 says, "Behold, how good and how pleasant it is / For brothers to dwell in unity!" This verse speaks of the goodness and pleasantness of dwelling in unity. According to verse 2, such a dwelling in unity "is like the precious ointment upon the head, that ran down upon the beard, even Aaron's beard: that went down to the skirts of his garments" (KJV). Ointment spreads more slowly than oil does. In the church life the ointment does not run; rather, it spreads slowly, gradually, and gently. The precious ointment spreads from Aaron's head even to the skirts of his garments. This indicates that it comes down from the Head to the entire Body.

In verse 3 the dwelling in unity is likened to the dew of Hermon and to the dew "that came down upon the mountains of Zion." Hermon, a high mountain, signifies the heavens, from which the dew descends. The mountains are the local churches, and the dew is the grace of Christ. This dew that descends upon the local churches is very refreshing. We can testify that the refreshing element of Christ descends upon us in the local churches. Praise the Lord for the heavenly dew that descends upon the local churches for our enjoyment!

The ointment and the dew bring in life. Verse 3 says, "There Jehovah commanded the blessing: / Life forever" (v. 3). Note that this verse does not say, "Jehovah gave the blessing"; it says, "Jehovah commanded the blessing." In the church life as the house of God, we enjoy the commanded blessing of life.

Even in Old Testament times, when God's people came to a material temple, they enjoyed a wonderful life in the house of God. They gathered together around the temple and offered the top portion of the rich produce of the good land. Then they enjoyed these offerings with God and in the presence of God. This was their life, their living, and their worship. They worshipped the Lord through enjoying the riches of the good land. Because this was their living, they were planted and flourished in the house of the Lord. This is a picture, in typology, of what can happen on the ground of oneness.

GOD'S REQUIREMENT

The ground of oneness is not simply a matter of one city, one church. The ground of oneness is deeper, richer, higher, and fuller than this. We all must learn that in this universe God has chosen only one place, and that place is the church. God requires us to go to this place He has chosen. Spiritually speaking, we must destroy every place other than the church and every name other than the name of Christ. This means that we must destroy our culture and religious background. You were born in a particular region of this country. You need to destroy the influence of that place. Perhaps you had a religious background in a particular denomination. Now you must destroy that denominational place within you. The places that we must destroy include our disposition, temperament, and habits. We must destroy everything that damages the oneness of the one new man.

According to Colossians 3:11, in the new man "there cannot be Greek and Jew, circumcision and uncircumcision, barbarian, Scythian, slave, free man, but Christ is all and in all." The church with Christ is the unique place of God's choice. In order to fulfill the word of Colossians 3:11, every other place must be utterly destroyed. We must destroy everything that is not the church with Christ. Then we will simply be in the church life enjoying Christ as the riches of the good land. As we enjoy Him with God, we will be planted in the house of the Lord, we will grow, and we will flourish. This is the proper way to have the Christian life and the church life. This is the ground of oneness.

On this ground it is not possible to have division, for the basis of division has been destroyed. Our temperament, disposition, natural characteristics, and preferences have all been eliminated. Our religion, culture, and particular ways have also been destroyed. Having destroyed all the pagan places, we simply go to the place of God's choice.

The church life has been weakened because of the lack of willingness to destroy the heathen places. Deuteronomy 12 has great spiritual significance for us today. In our human life and culture there are many places that remain to be destroyed. We must destroy them all and then go to the unique place of God's choice, the church. In the church there cannot be anything other than Christ. Christ must be all and in all. It is easy to say this, but it is not easy to practice it in a definite way. Nevertheless, we have no excuse for not practicing this principle.

In every place that is to be destroyed there is a dedicated pillar, a symbol, or an image. This means that even in our character or disposition there may be such pillars, symbols, or images. Therefore, we must destroy all the places with their pillars, symbols, and images. Do not preserve any place. Rather, destroy them and go to the place of the Lord's choice. As we have pointed out again and again, this place is the church. Having come to the church, we should have nothing other than the person of Christ and the unique way of the cross. Then we will enjoy Christ in the church as the top portion of the rich produce of the land. As we enjoy Him before God, this enjoyment will become our worship, our church life, and even our Christian daily living. Then we will grow and mature on the ground of oneness.

CHAPTER SIX

THE BLESSING OF LIFE
UNDER THE ANOINTING OIL
AND THE WATERING DEW
ON THE GROUND OF ONENESS

(1)

Scripture Reading: Psa. 133:1-3; John 17:21-23; Eph. 3:16—4:6;
1 John 2:27; 1 Pet. 3:7

The truth of oneness is great and profound. The full meaning of the genuine oneness revealed in the Bible is far beyond our apprehension. Because it is difficult for us to understand the oneness unfolded in the Scriptures, the Lord Jesus prayed about oneness in John 17 instead of speaking about it as the continuation of His discourse to His disciples. I believe that the Lord Jesus realized that His disciples were not able to understand the matter of oneness. Therefore, He offered a prayer regarding it.

John 17 is a deep, profound, mysterious composition. This chapter is itself definite evidence that the Bible is inspired by God. No human being could compose such a writing as the seventeenth chapter of John. During the past fifty years I have come back to this chapter again and again. However, I must admit that I have touched only a fraction of the truth found here.

ONE AS THE FATHER AND SON ARE ONE

Verses 21 through 23 are representative of the profoundness of this chapter. In verse 21 the Lord prayed, "That they all may be one; even as You, Father, are in Me and I in You, that they also may be in Us." What is the oneness spoken of in this verse? What does it mean for us to be one even as the Father is in the Son and the Son is in the Father? Surely this oneness is beyond our understanding. In verse 22 the Lord went on to say, "The glory which You have given Me I have given to them, that they may be one, even as We are one." What is the glory which the Father has given to the Son and which the Son has given to us? Furthermore, what does it mean for us to be one even as the Father and the Son are one? Some may think that this oneness is simply a matter of the three persons of the Divine Trinity having no dispute, argument, or dissension. According to this concept of oneness, to be one means to be in harmony and to have no disagreements. Those who understand verse 22 in this way would say that if a good number of believers can come together without argument or dissension, they are one just as the Father and the Son are one.

This understanding of oneness is too superficial. Surely the oneness here is not merely that of individual units coming together in harmony and agreement. Here the Lord said that He has given us the very glory the Father has given Him in order that we may be one in the Father and the Son. This points to a oneness that exists in the divine nature and the Divine Being. The three of the Triune God are one in Their nature and being.

The oneness of the believers in Christ should be essentially the same. The use of the word *glory* here substantiates this. Because we have received from the Son the very glory He has received from the Father, we may be one even as the Father and the Son are one. This points to a oneness that is not the mere addition of individual units but a oneness that is related to nature and being. Otherwise, the word *glory* would not be used in this verse. Glory is the very factor of the oneness here. The glory has been given to us in order that we may be one even as the Father and the Son are one. Hence, the glory of the Divine Being is the factor of the oneness among those who believe in Christ.

Verse 23 says, "I in them, and You in Me, that they may be perfected into one." Once again we see that this is not a mere oneness of addition. The believers are not simply added together to be one. Verse 23 is even stronger than verses 21 and 22 regarding oneness, for it speaks of our being perfected into one. This indicates that we may be one, but our oneness may be just at the beginning stage. It may not have yet grown or reached perfection.

Although we can point out certain things about these verses, we cannot understand them adequately. Furthermore, it is difficult for us, even after we have read them again and again, to state the main point in each verse. This proves that the oneness about which the Lord prayed in this chapter is profound and far beyond our comprehension.

THE MINGLING OF THE TRIUNE GOD WITH THE BELIEVERS

In the Bible there are four great chapters on the matter of oneness: Deuteronomy 12, Psalm 133, John 17, and Ephesians 4 with the last part of Ephesians 3. It is a great loss and a frustration of understanding to separate Ephesians 4:1-6 from 3:16-21. It is very helpful, however, when all these verses are read together as one unit. The oneness spoken of in 4:1-6 is intimately related to what is covered in 3:16-21. The word *therefore* in 4:1 indicates this. It shows that these verses in chapter 4 are the result of what immediately precedes them in chapter 3. In 3:16-21 Paul prays that the Father would grant us to be strengthened through His Spirit into the inner man, that Christ may make His home in our hearts, that we, being rooted and grounded in love, may be strong to apprehend with all the saints what the breadth and length and height and depth are and to know the knowledge-surpassing love of Christ, that we may be filled unto all the fullness of God. The result is that, according to the power which operates in us, there is glory to God in the church and in Christ Jesus. In light of all this, Paul declares in 4:1, "I beseech you therefore, I, the prisoner in the Lord, to walk worthily of the calling with which you were called." As the context makes clear, to walk worthily of our calling is mainly to keep the oneness of the Spirit. In verses 4 through 6 Paul goes on to point out that the oneness of the Spirit is the very Triune God. Paul speaks of the Body and of the one Spirit, the one Lord, and the one God and Father. The fact that the Body and the Triune God are mentioned together indicates that oneness is actually the mingling of the Triune God with the believers.

In Ephesians 3 Paul refers to the three of the Triune God. Paul prays that the Father would strengthen the saints through His Spirit into the inner man so that Christ may make His home in their hearts. Here we have the Father, the Spirit, and Christ (the Son). Then in chapter 4 Paul speaks of the Spirit, the Lord, and the Father. He refers to the Triune God in relation to the oneness of the Spirit and the Body. This indicates that oneness is not merely a matter of addition but of the mingling of the Triune God with the believers. Oneness is the mingling of the processed God with the believers.

Many references to the Triune God, especially in the Epistles, indicate the process through which God has passed. In the New Testament the Triune God—the Father, the Son, the Spirit—is revealed clearly in relation to the incarnation, human living, crucifixion, and resurrection of Christ. In Matthew 28:19 the Lord Jesus charged His disciples to disciple the nations and to baptize them "into the name of the Father and of the Son and of the Holy Spirit." Before the resurrection of Christ, people could not be baptized into the name of the Triune God. Only after God had been processed through Christ's incarnation, human living, crucifixion, and resurrection could believers be baptized into the name of the Father, Son, and Spirit. To be baptized, immersed, into this name of the processed God is to participate in the processed God. Furthermore, in the Epistles we see that the processed Triune God is for our participation and enjoyment. Therefore, eventually the Triune God becomes mingled with us. This mingling is the oneness.

The mere oneness of addition is very superficial. The oneness revealed in the Bible is the mingling of the processed Triune God with His chosen people. If we see this, then we can more easily understand the Lord's prayer concerning oneness in John 17. The oneness in John 17 is the mingling of divinity with humanity. However, we do not mean simply divinity in itself but divinity after it has been processed through incarnation, human living, crucifixion, and resurrection. Having passed through such a process, the Triune God becomes our portion and enjoyment. As the life-giving Spirit, He mingles Himself with those who believe in Christ.

With this concept of oneness in mind, let us come back to John 17:21. We have seen that here the Lord prayed that "they all may be one; even as You, Father, are in Me and I in You, that they also may be in Us." Here the Lord said that He is in the Father and that the Father is in Him. This no doubt indicates that the Father and the Son are mingled. This mingling is the oneness between the Father and the Son. The oneness between the Father and the Son is that the Father is in the Son and that the Son is in the Father. The Lord prayed that we would be one in the same way, even that we would be one "in Us," that is, in the Triune God.

ONENESS IN THE DIVINE GLORY

In verse 22 the Lord said that the glory which the Father had given Him He had given to His believers "that they may be one, even as We are one." Glory is the expression of God. This expression has been given to the Son. The Father has given the Son the glory to express Him in the divine life. Now this glory has been given to us by the Son so that we may be one, even as the Father and the Son are one. This oneness is the oneness in the divine glory for the corporate expression of God.

PERFECTED INTO ONE

In verse 23 the Lord continued, "I in them, and You in Me, that they may be perfected into one." Here we see the mingling of the processed God with the believers. The words *I, them,* and *You* refer respectively to Christ, the believers, and the Father. The Son is in the believers, and the Father is in the Son. This is the mingling of the Triune God with the believers. As a result of such a mingling, we may be perfected into one.

Perhaps you are wondering what it means to be perfected into one. On the day we believed in Christ, we came into this oneness. However, we still have problems with our natural man, our natural constitution, and our natural disposition. But the more we experience Christ as the life-giving Spirit, the more all these natural elements are reduced. As they are reduced through our experience of the Triune God, we are perfected into one.

We all need to be impressed with the fact that the oneness revealed in the Bible is not a matter of adding the believers together to form a harmonious unit. Such a concept of oneness is natural and superficial. Once again we say that oneness is the mingling of the processed Triune God with the believers. Having seen this oneness as it is unfolded in John 17 and Ephesians 4, let us now consider Psalm 133.

TWO ASPECTS OF ONENESS

This psalm is so profound that it is difficult to speak about it. Verse 1 says, "Behold, how good and how pleasant it is / For brothers to dwell in unity!" Notice that the psalmist uses two adjectives to describe brothers dwelling together in oneness. He says that this is good and pleasant. The reason two adjectives are used is that in the following verses the dwelling together in oneness is likened to two things: to the precious ointment on the head of Aaron and to the dew of Hermon on the mountains of Zion. These two adjectives point to two aspects of oneness. The oneness is good and pleasant: good as the precious ointment and pleasant as the descending dew.

Of these aspects, the first—Aaron—is a person, and the second—Zion—is a place. Have you ever seen that the church has these two aspects? On the one hand, the church is a person; on the other hand, the church is a place. As a person, the church includes the Head with the Body. As a place, the church is the dwelling place of God. Elsewhere in the Bible we see that the church is the bride, the new man, and the warrior. These, however, are aspects of the church as a person. Actually, the church has just two main aspects: the aspect of a person and the aspect of a dwelling place. Related to these two aspects of the church are the ointment and the dew.

THE SPREADING OINTMENT AND
THE DESCENDING DEW

Although in verse 2 the King James Version speaks of ointment, most other versions use the Hebrew word for *oil*. This oil refers to the anointing oil described in Exodus 30. That anointing oil was a compound ointment formed by blending four spices with olive oil. Aaron, his sons, the tabernacle, and everything related to the tabernacle were anointed with this ointment. According to Psalm 133, this ointment, this compound anointing oil, was upon a person, Aaron. We have pointed out that, by contrast, the refreshing, watering, and saturating dew was on a place, the mountains of Zion.

Neither the anointing oil nor the saturating dew moved quickly. The dew did not fall down like rain; it descended, came down, in a gradual way. In like manner, the ointment did not actually run down upon Aaron's beard; it spread upon his beard and then ran down to the hem of his garments. The Hebrew root means "to strew," as to strew over a surface. It also means "to spread," like to spread a cover, a bedspread, over a bed. Hence, the anointing oil upon Aaron's head spread upon his beard; it did not swiftly run down upon the beard. Gently and slowly, the ointment spread.

In the same principle the dew came down upon the mountains of Zion. In our hymnal there is a hymn about "showers of blessing" (#260). Such spiritual showers are somewhat Pentecostal in nature. I have a greater appreciation for the spreading of the ointment and the descending of the dew than for the showers of blessing. Showers are not related to oneness. The genuine oneness is constituted of the spreading ointment and the descending dew.

ANOINTED WITH
THE PROCESSED TRIUNE GOD

We have pointed out emphatically that real oneness is the mingling of the processed God with the believers. Although this is revealed in the New Testament, we do not see in the New Testament the way to practice this oneness. The way to practice this mingling is in Psalm 133. The ointment in verse 2 is a type of the processed Triune God who today is the all-inclusive compound Spirit. According to Exodus 30, the anointing oil is a compound formed by blending four spices with a hin of olive oil. This compound typifies the all-inclusive Spirit who is the processed God for our enjoyment. In this compound Spirit we have not only divinity but also Christ's humanity, the effectiveness of His death, and the power of His resurrection. In other words, the compound Spirit is the processed God with the divine attributes, the human virtues, the effectiveness of Christ's death, and the power of Christ's resurrection. In the church life this compound Spirit is continually anointing us.

The ointment can be compared to paint, and the anointing to the application of the paint. When you paint a chair, you may put on one coat of paint after another. As the compound Spirit anoints us, He "paints" us, and the "paint" is the very Triune God. In this "paint" we have the humanity of Christ, the effectiveness of Christ's death, and the power of Christ's resurrection. We also have Christ's divinity and human living. As all these ingredients of the ointment are applied to us, we are "painted" with the processed Triune God and with all the elements in the compound ointment. The proper church life is a life in the oneness that is the mingling of the processed Triune God with the believers. As we remain in this oneness, we are "painted" with the ointment. The more we are "painted" in this way, the more our natural constitution, temperament, and disposition are eliminated. What remains is the mingling of the processed Triune God with our uplifted humanity. This is the oneness.

In such a oneness it is not possible to have division, not even dissension. In this oneness there is no room even for our opinion. Although we need much more experience of the divine "painting" that brings us into oneness, we have had at least some experience of this in the church life. To a certain degree at least, we have all entered into the oneness.

When we were in the denominations or independent groups, we found it easy to be opinionated or critical. But in the church the dissenting element and divisive factors are subdued. This is the effect of oneness. The more the "paint" of the processed Triune God is applied to our being, the more difficult it is for us to be divided. Through the application of the heavenly "paint," we are brought into the genuine oneness, not the superficial oneness that is according to the natural concept. We are in the oneness that is the processed Triune God "painted" into our very being.

As we have pointed out, this ointment, this divine "paint" does not run down; it spreads. I want my house to be painted with paint that will stick, not with paint that will run down the walls like water. Likewise, when the ointment is applied to us, it sticks to our inner being; it does not run down. The running of the ointment is like the experiences in Pentecostalism or in the charismatic movement. Experiences of that kind pass quickly. In the church life, however, the spiritual blessing comes to us gradually, slowly, and gently. But once it comes, it remains. Once the "paint" is applied to us, it stays. After we have been coated with the anointing oil, the coat remains forever. Nothing can eradicate it.

The anointing does not cause us to have very much feeling in our emotion. Those experiences that come and go quickly, on the contrary, stir up our feeling. But this is not the normal experience in the church life. In the church life we experience the gradual spreading of the all-inclusive ointment. For example, in the church prayer meeting we may receive one or two "coats" of "paint" without having much feeling of it. As we have pointed out, this ointment has many ingredients. How grateful we are to the Lord for His recovery. Day by day in the church life, all the ingredients of the divine ointment are being wrought into us. Through the application of these ingredients to our inward being, we are spontaneously in the oneness. We find it exceedingly difficult to be divisive or even dissenting. How good, lovely, and enjoyable is the oneness in the church! The only way to be divisive is for us to make a strong decision contrary to our inner being. We are one spontaneously because we have been "painted" with all the elements of the heavenly "paint."

THE PROCESSED TRIUNE GOD APPLIED TO OUR BEING

The ground of oneness is simply the processed Triune God applied to our being. This is the oneness in which we find ourselves today. We are not in a oneness produced by adding together those who believe in Christ. In that kind of oneness it is just as easy to have subtraction as it is to have addition. However, once we have been brought into the oneness produced by the application of the processed Triune God to our being, it is very difficult to have any subtraction. This oneness is altogether different from the oneness in today's Christianity. The oneness in Christianity involves addition and subtraction. But the oneness in the churches in the Lord's recovery involves the application of the Triune God to our inward being.

FOR THE HEAD WITH THE BODY

The ointment is not for individuals; it is for the Body. It cannot be experienced by those who are separate and detached from the Body. According to the picture in Psalm 133, the ointment is upon the head. Then it spreads to the beard and goes down to the hem of the garment. This indicates that if we are individualistic, we cannot experience the ointment. Some may argue that they can contact the Lord alone at home. No doubt they can. The crucial matter, however, is whether or not we are one with the church. If we are one with the church, then we can properly contact the Lord alone at home. But if we separate ourselves from the church, our contact with the Lord will be altogether different. The reason is that the anointing oil is not for individualistic members; it is for the Head and the Body, even for the Head with the Body. Hence, to be "painted" by the ointment, we must be in the church. Then we spontaneously enjoy the application of the anointing oil with all its elements. How marvelous is the oneness produced by the application of this ointment!

GRACE—THE TRIUNE GOD
AS OUR LIFE SUPPLY FOR OUR ENJOYMENT

According to Psalm 133:3, the oneness is also like the dew that descends upon the mountains of Zion. The anointing oil is upon the person, Aaron, but the dew is upon the place, Zion. The dew signifies the grace of life (1 Pet. 3:7). The grace of life is the supply of life. In the church life we are not only under the anointing; we also receive the supply, the grace, of life. As we are anointed, we are also graced.

Suppose two brothers who live together in a brothers' house are having difficulty getting along. However, through their participation in the church life, they are graced and receive the supply of life. Spontaneously they will not only bear one another but truly love one another. This is the experience of the dew, the grace.

The apostle Paul abundantly experienced the Lord's grace. Three times he prayed that the "thorn" that was afflicting him would be removed. The Lord replied that His grace was sufficient for Paul. By this word the Lord indicated that He would not take away the thorn, but He would supply Paul with His sufficient grace.

In 2 Corinthians 13:14 Paul blesses the church with the words, "The grace of the Lord Jesus Christ and the love of God and the fellowship of the Holy Spirit be with you all." This verse indicates that grace is the Triune God processed to be our life supply. Whereas the ointment signifies the processed Triune God who is "painted" into our being, the dew signifies the Triune God who is our life supply for our enjoyment. Therefore, in the church life daily we are anointed and graced. We are "painted" with the processed God, and we are graced with the very same processed God as our life supply. This anointing and this supply make it possible for us to live in oneness. In the words of Psalm 133, this oneness is like the anointing oil and the watering dew. Under the anointing oil and the watering dew, we experience the blessing of life on the ground of oneness.

CHAPTER SEVEN

THE BLESSING OF LIFE
UNDER THE ANOINTING OIL
AND THE WATERING DEW
ON THE GROUND OF ONENESS

(2)

Scripture Reading: Psa. 133:1-3; John 1:14, 16-17; Acts 4:33; 11:23; 13:43; 14:26; Rom. 5:2, 17, 20-21; 1 Cor. 15:10; 2 Cor. 1:12; 9:8, 14; 12:9; 13:14; Eph. 2:7; 1 Tim. 1:14; 1 Pet. 3:7; 4:10; 5:10a; Gal. 6:18; Rev. 22:21

According to the New Testament, the oneness of the believers, or of the church, is mysterious, for it is intimately related to the processed Triune God. John 17:21-23 indicates that the believers are to be one in the Triune God just as the Father is in the Son and the Son is in the Father. By being in the Triune God, the believers are one. Furthermore, John 17:22 says that the glory the Father has given to the Son has been given by the Son to the believers so that they may be one even as the Father and the Son are one. Then verse 23 goes on to speak of being perfected into one. When we believed, we entered into this mysterious oneness. Now we must go on to be gradually perfected into this very oneness.

THE MINGLING OF THE TRIUNE GOD
WITH THE BODY OF CHRIST

In Ephesians 4:4-6 Paul lists seven aspects of oneness: one Body, one Spirit, one hope, one Lord, one faith, one baptism, and one God and Father. These verses also show the mysterious mingling of the Triune God with the Body of Christ. This mingling is the oneness of the believers. The Spirit in verse 4 is no doubt the compound, all-inclusive Spirit who is within the Body and gives life to the Body. According to 1 Corinthians 12:13, the Body came into existence through the baptism of this all-inclusive Spirit. Having been baptized in one Spirit, we must go on to drink of this Spirit. This indicates that the existence of the Body depends on the all-inclusive life-giving Spirit. Furthermore, the Body continues to exist through our drinking of this Spirit. Anything we drink becomes mingled with our inward being, with our blood and with the very fiber of our organic tissue. It is the same with the life-giving Spirit.

In Ephesians 4:5 Paul puts together the one Lord with the one faith and the one baptism. We get into the Lord through faith and baptism. To have faith in the Lord means to believe into Him. Of course, to be baptized into Him is to be put into Him. When we believed into Him and were baptized into Him, we became one with Him; that is, we were mingled with Him.

In verse 6 Paul says, "One God and Father of all, who is over all and through all and in all." The one God and Father is over all objectively, through all in a way that is partly objective and partly subjective, and in all subjectively. Hence, the Spirit is mingled with the Body, the Body is in the Lord, and the Father is over all, through all, and in all. This is a picture of the mingling of the Triune God with the Body of Christ. In this oneness we have the one hope, the hope of our coming glorification.

This oneness is altogether different from the oneness in today's Christianity, which is a mere oneness of addition. Such a oneness of addition can also lead to subtraction. The oneness revealed in the Bible is the mingling of the processed Triune God with His chosen people. Hence, the oneness in the Scriptures is a mingling of persons, a mingling of the divine person, the Triune God, with human persons who believe in Christ. The Triune God who is mingled with us has passed through the process of incarnation, human living, crucifixion, and resurrection. That genuine oneness referring to such a marvelous mingling is the clear revelation in John 17 and Ephesians 4.

A TYPE OF THE GENUINE ONENESS

We thank the Lord that for nearly all the spiritual things in the New Testament there are types in the Old Testament.

One of the types of genuine oneness is found in Deuteronomy 12. In this chapter the good land typifies the all-inclusive Christ, whereas the mountains, hills, and flourishing trees typify various centers of worship. The offerings mentioned in this chapter typify various aspects of the riches of Christ. Yes, Deuteronomy 12 is a record of a charge given to the children of Israel upon entering into the good land. But the details of this charge are also types, not only instructions that were to be taken literally by God's people at the time. We may use the passover lamb as an illustration of something that has both a literal and typical significance. The very lamb that was slain at the time of the passover is also a type of Christ as our Redeemer. In the same principle, the manna eaten by the children of Israel in the wilderness is a type of Christ as our heavenly food. This principle also applies to the good land in Deuteronomy 12. The land was not only a physical realm possessed by the children of Israel; it is also a type of the all-inclusive Christ. In this chapter God's chosen people were commanded to go to the unique place of God's choice. This place was selected in order to preserve the oneness of the children of Israel. This place was not only an actual location in the land of Canaan but is also a type of the genuine oneness of the believers in Christ today.

THE CORPORATE CHRIST

In Psalm 133 the oneness of God's people is likened to the precious ointment and to the watering dew. The precious ointment upon Aaron's head spread upon the beard and eventually went down to the hem of his garment. This picture of oneness is related to a person, Aaron, a type of Christ in His priestly ministry. As the High Priest, Christ served God, accomplished God's purpose, and fulfilled the desire of God's heart. However, in Psalm 133 Aaron typifies not only Christ Himself but Christ with His Body. This means that here Aaron typifies the corporate Christ, the Head with the Body. The church in a very real sense is the corporate Christ. The church is thus a universal, great person with a number of aspects: the aspects of the Body, the bride, the new man, and the warrior. All these aspects of the church are related to the person.

THE MANY LOCAL CHURCHES

In Psalm 133 the oneness of God's people is also likened to the dew of Hermon that descends upon the mountains of Zion. These mountains typify the local churches. Every local church is a mountain of Zion. There is one Zion but many mountains, signifying the many local churches. As a person, the church is uniquely one. As a place, the church, on the one hand, is the unique Zion; but, on the other hand, it is the many mountains of the one Zion. Although there is one church in the universe, there are nevertheless many local churches. Each local church is a peak among the many mountains of Zion. Therefore, the person is universal, but the mountains are local. Our oneness is like the precious ointment upon Aaron and like the dew upon the mountains of Zion. God's dwelling place, the temple, was located in Zion. On the one hand, the church is a person; on the other hand, it is a place. Upon the person there is the ointment, and upon the place there is the dew.

THE ULTIMATE CONSUMMATION
OF THE PROCESSED TRIUNE GOD

The fine oil in Psalm 133 is the ointment described in Exodus 30. This ointment is a picture of the compound, all-inclusive life-giving Spirit with the elements of divinity, humanity, human living, the effectiveness of Christ's death, and the power of Christ's resurrection. This all-inclusive Spirit is the expression of the processed God. I am burdened of the Lord to speak about this matter again and again until we are all deeply impressed with it.

In the first chapter of the Gospel of John, we are told that the Word, which was in the beginning with God and which was God, became flesh and tabernacled among us, full of grace and reality (vv. 1, 14). This Word, Christ, lived on earth for thirty-three and a half years. Then He passed through crucifixion and in resurrection became the life-giving Spirit. The life-giving Spirit is the ultimate consummation of the processed God. In John 14 through 16 we see that the Lord Jesus was one with the Father. To see Him was to see the Father (14:9). In 14:10 the Lord Jesus said, "Do you not believe that I am in the Father and the Father is in Me? The words that I say to you I do not speak from Myself, but the Father who abides in Me does His works." As the Lord spoke, the Father worked. In this chapter the Lord went on to tell the disciples that the Spirit of reality actually was He Himself realized. This means that when the Spirit indwelt the disciples, the Lord Himself was indwelling them. Hence, the Father, the Son, and the Spirit are the unique Triune God.

Passing through the various steps of a process, this very Triune God has become the all-inclusive Spirit. John 7:39 says, "The Spirit was not yet, because Jesus had not yet been glorified." The Spirit promised in chapters 14 through 16 is the Spirit referred to in 7:39. By receiving the Spirit as the ultimate consummation of the processed Triune God, we are one with the Triune God. For this reason, after speaking of the Spirit in chapter 14, the Lord went on to say in chapter 15 that if we abide in Him, He will abide in us. According to 14:23, if we love the Lord, the Father and the Son will come to us and make an abode with us. This abode is a mutual abode for the Triune God to abide in the believers and for the believers to abide in the Triune God. This mutual abiding is a matter of mingling.

After speaking the words recorded in John 14 through 16, the Lord Jesus offered the prayer to the Father recorded in chapter 17. The language of this prayer is altogether divine. In this prayer the Lord referred to the wonderful and mysterious mingling of the processed Triune God with the believers. Once again we point out that this mingling is the oneness.

THE ELEMENT OF OUR ONENESS

This oneness is made real and practical by means of the anointing that is upon Christ the Head and that spreads upon the Body. As long as we remain in the Body, we share the ointment. In this ointment we are one. Hence, the anointing of the compound, all-inclusive, life-giving Spirit is the element of our oneness. This means that to be one as members of the church is to be under the Spirit's anointing. If we are not under this anointing, we cannot be one with anyone, not even with ourselves.

Oneness does not depend upon our natural ability to get

along with others. Some believers may even be proud of having the kind of disposition that makes it easy for them to be one with other people. However, this kind of oneness is not the precious oneness revealed in the Bible. Actually, it is a very distasteful and uncomely sort of oneness. A person who boasts of this kind of oneness actually is not able to be one with others over a long period of time. On the contrary, he may eventually cause a great deal of disturbance. Genuine oneness consists in the anointing of the compound, all-inclusive Spirit as the ultimate consummation of the Triune God. Only under such an anointing do we have a genuine, unchanging oneness. Thousands of us can testify of the oneness we enjoy under the anointing of the compound Spirit. Our oneness has its source in the mysterious mingling of the processed Triune God with the believers. As we pointed out in the foregoing chapter, the more we are coated with the compound ointment, the more we are one. Praise the Lord that the all-inclusive Spirit is continually "painting" us!

DWELLING ON ONE OF THE "PEAKS"

The person aspect of the church is practical, but the place aspect is even more practical. Regarding the church as the universal person, we may not have any problems. However, concerning the church as the local mountains of Zion, we may have problems, for we may not be happy with the church in our locality, and we may desire to move elsewhere. But if we move to another city, we soon find the same problems in that place. The reason is that we ourselves are the same and that we are the cause of the problem. Some have assured me that they would never leave the church life. Nevertheless, discontent where they are, they like to have their choice of a "mountain." I can testify that as far as I am concerned, every "mountain" is the same. No matter where I am, I still praise the Lord and experience His work of transformation.

Those who move from place to place may love the universal church, but they have problems with the local church. They may declare that they have seen the Body of Christ and that they love the Lord's recovery. However, no matter in what locality they reside, they always have some difficulty with that "peak" of Zion. They may imagine that a church in a particular locality is outstanding. But as soon as they move there, they are disappointed, finding it no better than the "mountain" from which they have just moved. There is no need for us to move from "mountain" to "mountain." We should simply dwell on one of the peaks of Zion and enjoy there the descending dew of Hermon.

DEW—THE GRACE OF LIFE

In typology Hermon signifies the heavens, the highest place in the universe, and the dew signifies the grace of life (1 Pet. 3:7). Without the New Testament, it would be difficult for us to realize that dew signifies grace. Every Epistle written by Paul opens with a word about grace and closes with some mention of grace. When I was a young Christian in the denominations, I was told that grace denotes unmerited favor. According to this understanding of grace, to receive grace is to receive something that we do not deserve. Many Christians regard such unmerited favor as all the material blessings they receive from the Lord. For example, at the end of the year, some may count all the blessings God has given them that year: a good job, a bigger home, a late-model automobile. However, according to Paul's word in Philippians 3:8, everything apart from Christ is "refuse." He would regard things such as a job, a house, and an automobile as nothing but "refuse" in comparison to Christ. The grace spoken of in the Scriptures does not refer to mere material blessing. As many verses in the New Testament make clear, grace is the processed God as the life supply to be our enjoyment.

Strictly speaking, *grace* is a New Testament term. When used in the Old Testament, it has the meaning of "favor." According to John 1:17, grace came through Jesus Christ. When the Word became flesh and tabernacled among us, grace came also. This means that grace came with the incarnated God. Before the incarnation of Christ, grace had not come. Grace came through incarnation.

Many verses in Acts speak of grace. Acts 4:33 says, "With great power the apostles gave testimony of the resurrection of the Lord Jesus, and great grace was upon them all." This verse indicates that the great power in resurrection was the great grace. Christ in resurrection is grace. Such a grace is not a good house, job, or automobile. It is God experienced, received, enjoyed, and gained by the believers. In Acts 11:23 we are told that in Antioch Barnabas saw the grace of God. He, of course, did not see material blessings; he saw that the believers in Antioch were experiencing God in Christ as their life supply for their enjoyment.

In 1 Corinthians 15:10 Paul says, "By the grace of God I am what I am; and His grace unto me did not turn out to be in vain, but, on the contrary, I labored more abundantly than all of them, yet not I but the grace of God which is with me." We may compare this verse to Galatians 2:20, where Paul says, "It is no longer I who live, but it is Christ who lives in me." It was not Paul himself who labored more than the other apostles; it was the grace of God which was with him. This grace by which Paul labored more than others was no doubt Christ Himself as the life power and life supply to Paul in his experience.

In Romans 5:2 Paul says that through Christ "we have obtained access by faith into this grace in which we stand." The standing about which Paul is speaking here certainly is not something such as a house or a job. It is the Triune God who has been processed to become the all-inclusive Spirit as His ultimate consummation. Through Christ we can stand in the all-inclusive Spirit.

In Romans 5:17 Paul goes on to say that "those who receive the abundance of grace and of the gift of righteousness will reign in life through the One, Jesus Christ." If we have abundant grace, we will be able to reign in life. This verse implies that grace is life and that life is grace. In 1 Peter 3:7 Peter speaks of the grace of life, the inheritance of both a husband and wife. In Romans 5:21 Paul speaks about grace reigning unto eternal life. All these verses indicate that grace is nothing less than Christ as our life power and life supply for our experience and enjoyment.

If we are clear about this, we can have a greater appreciation of the dew as a type of Christ in Psalm 133. As the dew, the grace, becomes our enjoyment, we share in the genuine oneness. However, if we are not under the dew that waters, refreshes, and saturates us, we cannot be one with other believers. It is on the mountains of Zion that we experience this dew. If we would enjoy the dew, which typifies the all-inclusive grace, we must be on one of the peaks, the mountaintops, of Zion.

EXPERIENCING GRACE

Although many of us have experienced grace, we still do not know grace. What a pity! It is possible to know only in a doctrinal way that Christ is our life supply for our enjoyment. We need to know grace experientially.

Suppose a brother is having a problem with his wife. If he consults a pastor in Christianity, the pastor may exhort him with Paul's words about husbands and wives in Ephesians 5. The pastor then may proceed to advise the brother or to admonish him with respect to his wife. Such instruction, however, is altogether void of grace. What this brother needs is for someone to minister life to him and to pray with him. In this way, grace will be supplied to him, and he will be able to face the situation with his wife.

All married brothers and sisters must learn to go to the Lord and pray, "Lord, I need You. I cannot bear this situation any longer." Simply by opening to the Lord in this way, grace is dispensed into us. Through such a supply of grace, we are able to go on.

Recently, a brother testified how the situation between him and his wife reached a stalemate. He rarely spoke to her, and she rarely spoke to him. One day he asked his wife to pray with him. After that time of prayer, everything was changed. This is a testimony of the Lord's grace.

The brothers who live together may experience friction and feel that living in a brothers' house is unbearable. When the brothers feel this way, they should go to the Lord, contact Him, and tell Him that they cannot bear their living situation any longer. As they pray in this way, the supply of grace will come to them.

A situation that took place in the church in Chefoo more than forty years ago illustrates the sufficiency of the Lord's grace. Two brothers had a serious disagreement regarding finances. One brother claimed that the other owed him a certain amount of money. The other brother denied the first brother's claim. Eventually, they brought the problem to the elders of the church who endeavored to straighten out the situation. However, no solution came forth. On the contrary, the brothers even argued in the presence of the elders. Eventually, I told these two brothers that whoever received the Lord's grace would be willing to forget the debt altogether. I said that the "court" in the church is completely different from a worldly court. The difference is that the church "court" cares not for who is right or who is wrong; rather, it supplies grace to meet the need. If you receive the Lord's grace, you will praise Him and be willing to regard the matter as settled. The two brothers and the elders were surprised. Then I suggested that we all pray together. After a time of prayer, the two brothers began to weep and then to praise the Lord. Eventually, they were willing to let everything go, and there was no further problem. Instead, we all feasted on the Lord's grace.

ENJOYING GRACE IN THE CHURCH LIFE

In the local churches we are daily under the dew, under the grace. Whether we are married or single, old or young, we are under the dew that descends upon the mountains of Zion. Oh, how we enjoy the Lord's sufficient, exceeding, manifold, abundant grace! This grace is the very Lord Jesus Christ Himself as our life supply. If we wish to enjoy this grace in full, we need to be in the church life. According to Psalm 133, the grace does not descend upon the homes of individual believers; it descends upon the mountains of Zion, which typify the local churches. Thus, if we would enjoy the dew that descends from Mount Hermon, we need to be on one of the peaks of Zion. If those two brothers in Chefoo had separated themselves from the church life, they would have cut themselves off from the Lord's grace. Instead of having their problem settled through the Lord's grace in the church, they would have probably tried to settle it in a worldly court of law. Lacking the grace of the Lord, they would have continued to argue with one another according to right and wrong. But because they remained in the church life, the heavenly dew descended upon them, and they enjoyed a wonderful solution to their problem. In the church life the dew descends upon us richly. We are happy because we have the abundant supply of the all-sufficient grace.

The anointing oil and the watering dew are found in the church. Here we experience the anointing, the "painting," of the processed Triune God. Simultaneously, we enjoy the processed God as grace, as the life supply for our enjoyment. By this grace we can live a life that is impossible for people in the world to live. The brothers can love their wives to the uttermost, and the sisters can submit to their husbands in a full way. Such a living is possible through the grace we receive on the mountains of Zion.

We should never underestimate the importance of the church as a corporate person who receives the ointment and as the place under the descending dew. If we separate ourselves from the church in these two aspects, we have no further share in the anointing, and we are finished with the enjoyment of the dew. Other Christians may criticize us for bearing such a testimony concerning the church life. They may accuse us of narrowness and support their accusation with a word about God's omnipresence. These believers may say that as long as they pray and read the Bible, they can experience the Lord in a full way outside the church life. However, many of us can testify of the difference it makes to be in the church. Yes, we can pray and read the Word alone at home. When we do this, we receive a certain amount of grace. This measure of grace, however, is not as sweet, rich, powerful, inspiring, or sufficient as the grace we receive in the church. I can testify that, no matter whether the meetings of the church are high or low, rich or poor, I experience the ointment and the dew whenever I come to the meetings. The more I come to the meetings, the more I am preserved in the Lord's grace. Those, on the contrary, who separate themselves from the church life, cut themselves off from the full supply of grace. Apart from the Lord's mercy, they may find themselves wholly back in the world after a certain period of time.

Let us come to the church meetings, even when the meetings do not seem to be particularly rich. Simply by attending the meetings, we are preserved, for the dew still descends upon the mountains of Zion. Thus, simply by being in the meetings, we are under the watering dew. Our experience has confirmed this again and again.

EXPERIENCING TRUE ONENESS
AND PRESERVING IT

The oneness about which we have been speaking is the precious ointment upon Christ the Head and the refreshing dew that descends upon the mountains of Zion. It makes a tremendous difference whether we remain in this oneness or forsake it. Christians today feel free to come and go because they do not see this genuine oneness. They do not have the preserving and keeping element that the oneness affords. In His recovery the Lord has shown us that real oneness is the mingling of the processed Triune God with His chosen people. On the one hand, the processed God is the compound, all-inclusive Spirit that anoints us and "paints" us day by day. On the other hand, the processed God is the life supply for our enjoyment. Under this anointing oil and watering dew we experience true oneness. As long as we remain in the experience of the ointment and the dew, it is not possible for us to be divided. Rather, we are preserved in oneness. This is the meaning of Paul's word in Ephesians 4:3 about endeavoring to keep the oneness of the Spirit. Actually, this oneness is simply the all-inclusive life-giving Spirit Himself. We guard and preserve this oneness by remaining under the anointing oil and the watering dew.

CHAPTER EIGHT

THE DAMAGE AND LOSS
OF THE GROUND OF ONENESS

Scripture Reading: 1 Kings 11:6-8; 12:26-32; 13:33-34; 14:22-24; 15:14, 34; 22:43; 2 Kings 12:2-3; 14:3-4; 15:3-4, 34-35; 17:5-12, 18-23; 23:29-35; 2 Chron. 36:5-20; Psa. 137:1-6; 1 Cor. 1:10-13a; Rom. 16:17-18; Titus 3:10

In Deuteronomy 12 Moses charged the children of Israel to "completely destroy all the places where the nations whom you will dispossess have served their gods, on the high mountains and on the hills and under every flourishing tree" (v. 2). He also charged them to tear down their altars, crush their pillars, burn their Asherahs with fire, cut down the idols of their gods, and destroy their name from that place (v. 3). Having destroyed all these things, they were to come to the unique place of God's choice. According to 1 Kings, the temple was built in Jerusalem, the place God had chosen. It was the desire of God's heart for there to be a unique place for His presence. This one place protected God's people from division. Therefore, it was God's wisdom to require that all the places in which the nations served their gods be destroyed and that His people come to the unique place of His choice.

THE REBUILDING OF THE HIGH PLACES
AND THEIR SIGNIFICANCE

Although the children of Israel destroyed the places wherein the nations served their gods upon the mountains and hills and under the flourishing trees, and although the temple was built in Jerusalem, eventually the very things that had been destroyed came back. The high places (1 Kings 11:6-8; 12:31), the flourishing trees, the pillars, the Asherahs, and the idolatrous names were restored. In fact, Solomon, the very one who built the temple according to God's desire on the ground of oneness, took the lead to build up the high places once again (11:6-8). He built up again the very high places Moses had charged the people to destroy. These high places were related to fornication and idolatry. Solomon's setting up of the high places was especially connected with the indulgence of lust. It was for the sake of "all his foreign wives" that he built up the high places.

To set up a high place is to have a division. Hence, the significance of high places is division. God's intention with the children of Israel in the Old Testament was that His people be kept in oneness in order to worship Him in a proper way. To preserve the oneness of His people, God required that they come to the unique place of His choice. The high places, however, were a substitute and an alternative for this unique place. This indicates that division is a replacement for oneness. The unique place, Jerusalem, signifies oneness, whereas the high places signify division. Just as all manner of evil and abominable things were related to the setting up of the high places, so, in New Testament terms, all manner of evil is related to division.

RELATED TO LUST, AMBITION, AND IDOLATRY

According to the record in 1 Kings, two kings—Solomon, a good king, and Jeroboam, an evil king—took the lead to set up the high places. In the case of Solomon, the building of the high places was related to the indulgence of lust. Solomon had hundreds of wives and concubines. In order to satisfy their desire, he built up high places. His wives had "turned his heart after other gods" (11:4). In the case of Jeroboam, the building of the high places was related to ambition (12:26-32). Jeroboam wanted to maintain his empire. Fearing that the kingdom would return to the house of David if the people went to Jerusalem to worship, Jeroboam "made a house of high places" (v. 31). Hence, Jeroboam's ambition was the cause of his decision to build up high places. Furthermore, Jeroboam made two calves of gold and said to the people, "It is too much for you to go up to Jerusalem. Behold your gods, O Israel, who brought you up out of the land of Egypt!" (v. 28). He then "set one in Bethel, and he put the other one in Dan" (v. 29). Furthermore, "Jeroboam ordained a feast in the eighth month, on the fifteenth day of the month, like the feast that is in Judah" (v. 32). The month of this feast was "devised in his own heart" (v. 33). Jeroboam even appointed "priests from among the people who were not from the sons of Levi" (v. 31). What evil is associated with high places! The high places were related to lust, ambition, and idolatry. Since high places signify divisions, this indicates that the divisions among Christians today are related to these evil things.

Not many Christians realize that division is connected to lust, ambition, and idolatry. Most Christians would not go beyond saying that divisions are wrong and unscriptural and that they cannot agree with them. However, in the eyes of the Lord, division involves such things as lust, ambition, and idolatry. Remember, a high place is an elevation, something lifted above the common level. This indicates that a high place involves the exaltation of something. In principle, every high place, every division, in Christianity today involves the uplifting, the exaltation, of something other than Christ. The things that are exalted may not be evil. On the contrary, they may be very good and may include even Bible study or Bible teaching. Surely it is a good thing to teach the Bible. But Bible study may be related to division. In such a case, even a meeting for the study of the Scriptures becomes a high place; it may lead to the exaltation of something in place of Christ.

Today it is common for Christians to elevate things in place of Christ. For example, some elevate the practice of baptism by immersion. Although it is right and scriptural to immerse people, it is not right to exalt immersion in place of Christ. To do this is to build a high place for the exaltation of a particular mode of baptism. The existence of such a high place always gives an opportunity for the indulgence of lust or for the fulfillment of ambition. However, the unique place of God's choice kills our lust and restricts our ambition. Even a very good thing such as Bible study can open the way for lust and ambition to come in, if it is exalted above Christ. Lust is inevitably followed by idolatry. Ambition, in fact, is a form of idolatry.

When the children of Israel were about to cross the river Jordan and enter into the good land, Moses, out of his deep concern for them, charged them to destroy the heathen places of worship and to come to the unique place of God's choice. He issued this charge because he realized that this matter of the unique place of God's choice and the destroying of the heathen places was closely related to their destiny before God. If they were faithful to destroy the pagan centers of worship and to come to the place of God's choice, they would be doing what was right in the eyes of the Lord. But if they failed to comply with this demand, they would be doing what was evil in His eyes. When they entered the good land, God's people did destroy the high places and the names of the idols. Eventually, they were victorious in their battle to subdue the land. Men like Samuel and David are examples of those who absolutely followed God's command given through Moses.

During the reign of Solomon the temple was built in Jerusalem. As we are told in 1 Kings 8, the glory of the Lord filled the temple. The age of the building of the temple was a golden time in the history of the children of Israel. However, not long after the temple was built, Solomon, the one under whom it was constructed, began to rebuild the high places. As we have pointed out, he did this to please his wives and concubines. This indicates clearly that the rebuilding of the high places was related to Solomon's lust. Then, after the death of Solomon, Jeroboam, who was the rival of Rehoboam, king of Judah, built high places for the sake of his ambition. In both cases the building of the high places provoked God to wrath.

The account of the building of the high places under Solomon and Jeroboam is not merely a record of historical fact. This record has a spiritual significance, and it was written for our training. In Romans 15:4 Paul says, "The things that were written previously were written for our instruction." Hence, what was written concerning Solomon and Jeroboam was written for our spiritual instruction today.

A number of important matters are not covered in the New Testament in a full way. I believe that the Lord intends for us to consider these matters in the light of the types and figures presented in the Old Testament. For example, concerning the damage and loss of the ground of oneness, the New Testament does not say a great deal. Regarding this, there is not much development. Only three brief portions of the Word are devoted to it: 1 Corinthians 1:10-13, Romans 16:17-18, and Titus 3:10. However, in the types and pictures in the Old Testament, the matter of division is developed in a full and complete way. Just as we need to consult the record of the passover in Exodus to receive a full understanding of Christ as the Lamb of God, so we need to consider the record in Deuteronomy, 1 and 2 Kings, and 1 and 2 Chronicles to have a full understanding of division and of the damage and loss of the ground of oneness. According to the Old Testament record, division is caused by lust and ambition. Solomon is an example of the former, and Jeroboam is an example of the latter. The Old Testament also reveals that only the unique place of God's choice can deal with our lust and ambition. The reason so much emphasis is put on the matter of the place God has chosen is that only this place gives no opportunity for the indulgence of lust or the carrying out of ambition.

A WARNING

In 1 Kings 8 Solomon offered a marvelous prayer. As the one who wrote the Song of Songs, Solomon was very deep in spiritual things. Nevertheless, in 1 Kings 11 we see that Solomon's "heart turned away from Jehovah the God of Israel, who had appeared to him twice, and who had commanded him concerning this very matter, not to go after other gods" (vv. 9-10). However, Solomon "did not keep that which Jehovah had commanded" (v. 10). How far Solomon had fallen! His fall should be a warning to us. If we do not accept the restriction of God's choice, we also may fall in the same way Solomon did. In fact, this has been the experience of a number of saints who once had part in the Lord's recovery. They seemed to be very useful to the Lord in the building up of the church. At a certain stage, they were today's Solomon building the temple or writing the Song of Songs. But due to some kind of lust, they eventually became divisive. They set up a "high place" for the satisfaction of their lust. I have observed this both in China and in the United States.

HIGH PLACES AND AMBITION

In 1963 those from certain Christian groups proposed to meet jointly with us in Los Angeles. At the start of this joint meeting, I gave a message from Romans 14, warning the saints about divisions caused by different opinions. I pointed out that we all must learn the lesson of oneness according to Romans 14. Nevertheless, after a very short period of time, at least two "high places" were set up: a "high place" that elevated speaking in tongues and another high place that uplifted the teaching of biblical doctrine. Those involved in these "high places," these divisions, had not the least concern for the unique place of God's choice. In other words, they had no genuine concern for oneness. On the contrary, they cared only for the satisfaction of their desire, their lust. Furthermore, some became divisive because of ambition. As a result, ambitious to be leaders, they left the Lord's recovery. Because their ambition could not be fulfilled in the church life, they turned their back on the church and even began to oppose it. At first, they regarded the Lord's recovery very highly. But simply because their ambition for leadership was not fulfilled in the recovery, they left and set up a little "hill" to fulfill their ambition. This "hill," another "high place," was a cause of division.

It is crucial that we take heed to all the points in Deuteronomy 12. We must learn to fear the Lord our God and not to do what is right in our own eyes. Rather, fearing the Lord, we must do what is right in His eyes. Nothing requires us to fear God as much as the keeping of the oneness. If some Christians were to establish a place of worldly entertainment, we would immediately condemn that practice. However, not many would condemn just as vigorously the establishment of a divisive Christian meeting. At the most, the majority of Christians would say simply that they do not agree with that meeting. Some may even justify it, claiming that it helps people to know the Bible and to follow the Lord. Apparently, such a meeting is designed to render spiritual help. Actually, it is a division that has its source in someone's lust or ambition. At such a "high place" something other than Christ is exalted.

When I first went to Shanghai in 1933, I met a particular

brother who was very active in the church life. He had come into the church in 1927 and was one who sought the Lord. One day Brother Nee pointed out to me that this brother was ambitious to be an elder. Eventually, in 1948, seeing that his desire for eldership had not been fulfilled, he left the church. He started a meeting in his home and hired a traveling preacher to minister. He turned his back wholly against the church. Furthermore, the preacher hired by him wrote a long book criticizing and defaming Brother Nee and spreading rumors about him. After twenty-one years in the church life, this brother left the church in order to set up a certain kind of "high place."

NOT ELEVATING ANYTHING IN PLACE OF CHRIST

If you investigate the situation of today's Christianity, you will learn that every division is an elevation of some kind. It is good to teach the Bible. But Bible study should not become an elevation that separates God's people from one another. The same is true regarding pray-reading. You may find pray-reading very helpful. However, you should not elevate it by insisting on the practice of pray-reading in the meetings. If you elevate pray-reading, you will make even pray-reading a cause of division. We need to ask the Lord to grant us mercy that we may not elevate anything in place of Christ. If we hold to an attitude of elevating our opinion or preference, we set up a "high place," a place of division. This is what happened among some of those who desired to have that joint meeting in Los Angeles in 1963. Those who opposed speaking in tongues elevated their attitude and preference, whereas those who advocated it uplifted theirs. Neither group was willing to regard my word about caring for the feeling of others. They desired to have their own way. Such a desire led them to set up "high places."

All of us, especially the young people, must learn not to elevate anything other than the Lord Jesus. He alone should be exalted. In the church life we should not have any "high places." Instead, we should all be on one level to exalt Christ.

A MATTER OF GREAT SIGNIFICANCE

The high places built by Solomon and Jeroboam seriously damaged the ground of oneness. If this matter of the high places were not of great significance, the Old Testament would not mention it repeatedly. In 1 Kings 14:22 and 23 we are told that "Judah did what was evil in the sight of Jehovah" for "they also built for themselves high places and pillars and Asherahs on every high hill and under every flourishing tree." The word *every* used with respect to the high hills and the flourishing trees shows that this practice was common and very widespread. Once they were set up, these high places were not easily removed, even by good kings such as Asa. Although Asa did what was right in the eyes of the Lord and "removed all the idols that his fathers had made," the "high places were not removed; otherwise the heart of Asa was perfect with Jehovah all his days" (15:12, 14). The people might have excused or justified the existence of high places by saying that they did not use them for the worship of pillars or Asherahs but for sacrificing to God and for offering incense to Him. Regarding Jehoshaphat, we are told that "he walked in all the way of Asa his father; he turned not aside from it, doing what was right in the sight of Jehovah. Nevertheless the high places were not removed; the people offered sacrifices and burned incense still on the high places" (22:43). Furthermore, although Jehoash also did what was right in the sight of the Lord, the high places were not removed during his reign. Rather, "the people still sacrificed and burned incense in the high places" (2 Kings 12:3). Time and time again we are told that "the people still sacrificed and burned incense in the high places" (14:3-4; 15:3-4, 34-35).

RESTRICTED BY GOD'S CHOICE

If we had been there at the time, we might have taken sides with those who sacrificed at the high places. Those who went to the high places might have argued that it was inconvenient to travel the long distance to Jerusalem three times a year. Christians still use this kind of excuse today. It seems that for every division in Christianity an excuse is offered to justify it. Nevertheless, in Old Testament times the Lord would not accept anything offered to Him at the high places. He regarded any sacrifice offered there as an abomination in His sight, for it was presented in a place of division, in a place that opened the door for the indulgence of lust and gave opportunity for the pursuit of ambition. Only the worship, the offerings, and the incense at the place of God's unique choice were regarded as genuine. That place killed lust and gave no opportunity for ambition. Even to present a genuine offering in a place other than the unique place of God's choice creates an opportunity for the indulgence of selfish desire. Any "high place," even those at which genuine sacrifices are offered, causes damage to the ground of oneness. Those "high places" are used by people in their lust and ambition for the fulfillment of their own purpose.

From my experience in the Lord's recovery on the mainland of China, I can testify that the unique place of God's choice leaves no opportunity for the indulgence of lust or for the exercise of our ambition. During all the years in China, I was under the direction of Brother Nee's ministry. In all my preaching I was the same as he. All the "high places" were torn down, and therefore there was no room for the indulgence of lust or the carrying out of selfish ambition. The same is true among us today. We care only to exalt Christ. If we maintain the ground of oneness, God's unique choice, without elevating anything other than Christ, it will not be possible to have division. In the Lord's recovery we elevate Christ and Christ alone. We may talk a great deal about life, but we do not even elevate life to the point of making it a "high place." Certain brothers among us are very keen and have a good deal of natural ability. But their keenness and ability must be restricted by the ground of God's choice. This restriction will keep them from elevating something in place of Christ. We in the Lord's recovery can testify that, in contrast to today's Christianity, we have no "high places." In Christianity "high places" are found everywhere. Each denomination and independent group is an elevation, a "high place." As we have pointed out repeatedly, these elevations are all related to lust or ambition.

CARRIED AWAY INTO CAPTIVITY

According to the Old Testament record, after the ground of oneness was damaged, it was actually lost. Israel, the northern kingdom, was conquered by the Assyrians, and Judah, the southern kingdom, was conquered by the Babylonians. Because of the sin of Jeroboam in setting up the high places, the nation of Israel was led into captivity by the Assyrians. In His wrath God chose to cast them out of the Holy Land. Second Kings 17:22 and 23 say, "The children of Israel walked in all the sins of Jeroboam which he did; they did not depart from them, until Jehovah removed Israel from His sight." When the Israelites were in the Holy Land, they were in the Lord's presence. But when they were carried away to Assyria, they were cast out of the presence of the Lord.

Israel's captivity should have been a warning to Judah. The kingdom of Judah, however, did not heed this warning. As 2 Kings 17:19 says, "Judah also did not keep the commandments of Jehovah their God but walked in the statutes of Israel, which they had made." Those in Judah built up more high places and gave more opportunity for evil to come in. This forced the Lord to send in Pharaoh Neco (23:29-35). Pharaoh Neco removed Jehoahaz from the kingship and made Eliakim king, changing his name to Jehoiakim (v. 34). Jehoahaz was taken to Egypt, where he died. Because Judah would not remove the high places, the Lord eventually sent in the Babylonian army under Nebuchadnezzar. Eventually, the temple was destroyed, and a great many of the people were carried away into captivity.

Formerly, all the children of Israel were in the good land. They were one people with a unique center of worship in Jerusalem. First, they damaged this oneness by setting up high places throughout the land. But eventually they went on to lose this oneness through the invasion of the Assyrians and the Babylonians. Having been cast out of the good land, God's people became Egyptian Jews, Assyrian Jews, or Babylonian Jews. The ground of oneness had been lost absolutely.

Psalm 137:1-6 is a description of their plight in Babylon. God's people were in a strange land, and they could not sing the Lord's song. Instead, by the rivers of Babylon they sat down and wept when they remembered Zion. What a picture of the situation of Christians today! The vast majority of Christians have been carried away into captivity. The ground of oneness has not only been damaged—it has been fully lost. Very few Christians have any realization of what the ground of oneness is. As a result of their captivity, many of the children of Israel even forgot their language. They eventually became Egyptians, Assyrians, and Babylonians. This is a vivid portrait of today's Christianity. May the Holy Spirit speak more to us concerning the damage and loss of the ground of oneness.

CHAPTER NINE

THE RECOVERY AND TESTIMONY
OF THE GROUND OF ONENESS

Scripture Reading: Ezra 1:1-11; 2:1-2; 3:1-6, 8-13; 6:14-18; 7:6-9;
8:28-30; 9:1-7; 10:1; Psa. 126:1-6; Isa. 35:10; 51:11

In the foregoing chapter we saw that the high places caused the damage and the loss of the ground of oneness. Before Solomon and Jeroboam set up the high places, the children of Israel had been preserved in oneness by the temple in Jerusalem, the unique place of God's choice. At the time of the annual feasts, God's people gathered together in oneness. As they ascended Mount Zion, they even chanted the words of Psalm 133: "How good and how pleasant it is / For brothers to dwell in unity!" However, to indulge his lust, Solomon took the lead to build high places. These high places damaged the genuine oneness of God's people, for they hindered many from going up to Jerusalem to worship. Some might have gone to the high places under the pretense of worshipping God. Nevertheless, in the high places there were idols. Furthermore, in order to carry out his ambition, Jeroboam also set up high places. We are told that high places were set up on every high hill and under every flourishing tree. This indicates how widespread and common they were.

A PICTURE OF TODAY'S SITUATION

The high places were the source of all manner of evil. Since the high places signify division, this indicates that division is a source of evil. The high places came in through man's flesh and ambition. Solomon set up high places because of lust, whereas Jeroboam did so because of ambition. Hence, lust and ambition were the main factors of the building of the high places. In today's terms, division is the result of the flesh and of ambition. In Christianity today there are "high places" everywhere, for Christianity is filled with divisions. All these "high places" are elevations where something other than Christ is exalted. By this we see that the situation of today's Christianity is a definite fulfillment of the type in the Old Testament.

First, the oneness of God's people was damaged by the high places. This damage provoked God to wrath. Unable to tolerate the situation, He sent the Assyrian army to invade the northern kingdom of Israel. Israel's experience should have been a warning to Judah, the southern kingdom. Nevertheless, those in Judah went on worshipping at the high places. Although some were carried away to Egypt by Pharaoh Neco, the people refused to heed even this warning. Eventually, the Babylonian army not only conquered the land of Judah but also destroyed the temple and carried away a large number of people to captivity in Babylon. Furthermore, the vessels of the temple were taken to Babylon and put in the house of idols. Thus, the ground of oneness was not only damaged but fully lost.

This is a picture of the situation among today's Christians. The denominations and independent groups are "high places," divisions. In each of these "high places" something other than Christ is exalted. Even very good and spiritual things are elevated and used to cause division.

NO REASON FOR DIVISION

According to Romans 14, there is no reason for Christians to be divided. However, most Christians are accustomed to the existence of "high places." Some may even feel that today's "high places" are right and necessary. We think this way because we were born into an environment filled with division, with "high places" of every variety. Because we are so accustomed to division, we may have very little feeling about it. Paul's feeling in Romans 14, on the contrary, was altogether different. Here he encourages us not to argue over such things as eating or observing days. Concerning these things, we should refrain from expressing our opinion. In this way the oneness of the believers will be preserved.

In the previous chapter I referred to a joint meeting of Christian groups that was held for a while in Los Angeles in 1963. The members of these groups were eager to come together for the practice of the church life. Hearing of their interest and of their proposal to have a joint meeting, I gave them a word from Romans 14. I pointed out that if we intend to practice the church life, we must take the way set down by Paul in this chapter. Many Christians talk about the Body life in Romans 12, but they neglect the principles in Romans 14. Without Romans 14 it is impossible to have the Body life described in Romans 12. Throughout the centuries Christians have been divided by opinions over doctrine and practices. For example, Christians are divided over the matter of baptism. There is disagreement not only about the mode of baptism but also about the water that is used and the name in which believers are baptized. The opinions concerning baptism have caused many divisions, even many elevations that exalt a particular opinion. Therefore, it is of crucial importance that we follow the way exemplified by Paul in Romans 14. Those from these groups assured me that they would take this way.

Nevertheless, after just a few weeks, problems developed. Some insisted on playing tambourines and speaking in tongues in the meetings. Others strongly opposed these practices. Eventually, neither group was willing to give in and to care for the feeling of others in order to maintain oneness. Eventually, it was not possible for that joint meeting to continue. The ones in these groups expected everyone to be the same as they were. However, if we have such an expectation, it will not be possible to have the church life. The church life must be all-inclusive, able to include all manner of genuine Christians.

In Romans 14 Paul had no intention of taking sides on the questions of eating or of observing days. Instead, he said, "He who regards that day, regards it to the Lord; and he who eats, eats to the Lord, for he gives thanks to God; and he who does not eat, does not eat to the Lord, and he gives thanks to God" (v. 6). This was Paul's attitude, and it should be our attitude today.

We should not try to make everyone the same as we are. For example, although we may not speak in tongues, we should not forbid others to speak in tongues. On the other hand, those who speak in tongues should not insist that others do so as well. If we have this attitude, we will not be sectarian, and there will be no "high places" among us.

Some accuse us of narrowness. However, we are not narrow, for we receive all genuine Christians. The ones who are narrow are those who insist on a certain doctrine or practice. Their insistence on a particular matter causes it to be elevated and uplifted in place of Christ.

THE GROUND OF ONENESS UTTERLY LOST

All the divisions in Christianity are elevations that involve either lust or ambition. Division opens the way for every evil thing to come in. Consider the evil that Jeroboam did. He made two calves of gold and set one in Bethel and the other in Dan. He also made a house of high places and appointed priests of the high places from among all sorts of people. He "ordained a feast in the eighth month, on the fifteenth day of the month, like the feast that is in Judah, and he went up to the altar" (1 Kings 12:32). All these points can be applied to today's Christianity. For example, only genuine believers who have the life of Christ, who love the Lord, and who know the Word should be priests. But many of the ministers in Christianity today do not even believe that Christ is the Son of God. Furthermore, in Christianity there are many festivals, such as Christmas and Easter, that have been ordained and established by man. Furthermore, just as the children of Israel were eventually led into captivity and underwent a complete loss of the ground of oneness, so Christians today have been carried off to Babylon. The ground of oneness has not only been damaged; it has been utterly lost. Very few Christians have any idea of what the ground of oneness is. Who cares for the genuine oneness today? It is rare to find Christians who care about it. Generations ago, the genuine oneness of the believers in Christ was lost. For this reason the situation of today's Christianity is altogether Babylonian. Although some may talk about oneness, this is not the genuine oneness revealed in the Scriptures. When we speak of the ground of oneness, hardly anyone can understand our language. To most Christians, the language of oneness is a foreign tongue.

A RECOVERY OF ALL POSITIVE THINGS

The Old Testament reveals not only the damage and loss of the ground of oneness but also the recovery and testimony of this ground. Jeremiah prophesied that after seventy years of captivity in Babylon, the Lord would bring the people back to the good land. Jeremiah 29:10 says, "Thus says Jehovah, When seventy years are fulfilled for Babylon, I will visit you and establish My good word to you, to bring you back to this place." Ezra 1:1 refers to this prophecy of Jeremiah. Here we are told that in the first year of Cyrus the king of Persia, the Lord stirred up the spirit of Cyrus so that he made a proclamation throughout his kingdom regarding the building of the house of God in Jerusalem. This took place "that the word of Jehovah by the mouth of Jeremiah might be accomplished." This indicates that the return to Jerusalem was not initiated by man. According to the clear record of the Bible, it was initiated by God Himself.

When God's people were in Babylon, they did not offer sacrifice to Him there. Nowhere are we told that in Babylon they offered the burnt offering every morning and evening. No doubt, men like Daniel, Ezra, and Nehemiah prayed, but they did not have the ground to offer sacrifice to God. In Babylon there was no altar. Without an altar, it was impossible for them to offer anything to God. Moreover, in Babylon God's people could not observe the yearly feasts. What a pitiful situation! Babylon was a good place for fasting but not for feasting. It was suitable for weeping but not for rejoicing. Psalm 137:1 says, "By the rivers of Babylon, / There we sat down; indeed, we wept / When we remembered Zion." When the ground of oneness was lost, nearly everything else was lost also. God's people lost the riches of the good land, the altar, and the feasts. Only at the chosen place in Mount Zion could they enjoy all these marvelous things.

THE VESSELS AND THE ALTAR

When the Lord stirred up the spirits of the people to return to Jerusalem, not only was there a recovery of the ground of oneness; there was also a spontaneous recovery of all the positive things that had been lost. The vessels that Nebuchadnezzar "had brought out from Jerusalem and had put in the house of his gods" were brought back to Jerusalem (Ezra 1:7-11). Moreover, once the remnant of the people had returned, "they set up the altar upon its bases" (3:3). God's people knew that the place for the altar was not in Babylon but only in the unique place of God's choice in Jerusalem. The altar could not even be put in any place in the good land. It had to be set up on the very place Abraham offered Isaac to God on Mount Moriah. Anyone who wanted to present an offering to God had to go to that definite, specific, and unique place.

Today this unique place is the oneness. Whenever Christians lose the oneness, they automatically lose the place to set up the altar. As a result, they have no way to present a proper offering to the Lord. Before coming into the church life, many of us tried to offer ourselves to the Lord. I can testify that a number of times I consecrated myself to Him. But from our experience both before and after we came into the church life, we can testify that such a consecration was not genuine. Without returning to the unique ground of oneness, there is no way to offer anything to God. Soon after God's people had returned to Jerusalem, they set up the altar and began offering sacrifices again. It was the same in our experience. After we came into the church life, we found ourselves able to consecrate ourselves to the Lord in a proper and genuine way.

THE PROPER FUNCTION OF THE CONSCIENCE

Furthermore, it was after they returned from captivity that God's people dealt with their mixed marriages with the heathen (9:1-7). Their conscience could no longer tolerate such an ungodly practice. This was a spontaneous result of returning to the ground of oneness. Surely there were many mixed marriages among the people in Babylon. However, their conscience caused them to deal with these marriages only after they returned from captivity.

The same is true in the Lord's recovery today. After we came into the church life, our conscience began to function in a proper way. We "girded up our loins" and became careful regarding matters about which we had previously been rather loose. Before we came to the Lord's recovery, we might have been free to engage in certain worldly amusements. But after we came into the church life, our whole being was girded up. We began to pursue godliness, and we had an increased desire to pray and to read the Word. Spontaneously we exercised our conscience more thoroughly. This behavior was not the result of teaching or regulation. It was the automatic issue of returning to the ground of oneness. Simply because we had come into the church life, we had a desire for godliness. Many negative things began to drop off, and many positive things became our experience. For example, we had the sense within that we should no longer practice Christmas. No one charged us to discontinue the celebration of Christmas. We simply began to have the sense that we should no longer celebrate it. In like manner, we began to discard many other negative things and to enjoy positive things. This illustrates the fact that when the oneness is recovered, all the positive things are recovered along with it.

HOLY ASPIRATIONS

Nothing is more satisfying than the ground of oneness. For the Old Testament saints the thought of coming into the courts of the Lord's house stirred holy and godly aspirations within them. Many of the psalms illustrate this. These psalms are filled with aspirations of holiness, godliness, piety, and the presence of the Lord. In fact, even the thought of the house of God aroused such aspirations.

THE PRESENCE OF GOD

The presence of God is very much related to the ground of oneness. Before I came into the church life, I truly loved the Lord. However, I did not have much enjoyment of His presence. But when I came into the church life in a practical way, I began to enjoy the Lord's presence day by day. Even during the course of a very demanding job, I had the enjoyment of His presence. According to my experience, I can testify that participating in the church life makes a tremendous difference in our Christian life.

Many of us can give a similar testimony. Before we came to the church, we were in Babylon. We loved the Lord and we sought the Lord, but we did not have much enjoyment of His presence. However, after we came into the church life, various holy desires and aspirations were aroused within us. More than ever before, we aspired to be in the Lord's presence. This is the spontaneous result of returning to the ground of oneness, to the unique place of God's choice. When God's people returned to Jerusalem, all the positive things that had been lost during their captivity in Babylon were restored. All the sacred, godly, heavenly things spontaneously returned. It has been the same with us in the Lord's recovery today.

FILLED WITH REJOICING

Psalm 126:1-2 says, "When Jehovah turned again the captivity of Zion, / We were like those who dream. / At that time our mouth was filled with laughter / And our tongue with a ringing shout." God's returned people were filled with laughter and rejoicing because all the positive things had been restored. Before they returned to Jerusalem, however, they did not have such an enjoyment. But after they returned, they enjoyed so many excellent things that it seemed to them like a dream.

Isaiah 35:10 and 51:11, verses that are very similar, also speak of the joy of God's returned people. These verses declare that "the ransomed of Jehovah will return / And will come to Zion with a ringing shout, / And eternal joy will be upon their heads." The fact that this matter is repeated shows its importance, for anything in the Bible that is repeated is of special significance. During Isaiah's time, the Babylonian captivity had not yet occurred. Nevertheless, Isaiah spoke about the gladness, the enjoyment, of God's salvation of His ransomed people. He foresaw the joy of the returned captives. I do not believe that Solomon and his contemporaries were as joyful as Zerubbabel, Joshua the priest, Ezra, and all the others who had returned to Jerusalem from captivity. They experienced much more of the joy of God's salvation than Solomon did. For this reason, the writer of Psalm 126 declared that they were like those who dream.

THE ALL-INCLUSIVE ONENESS

How we thank the Lord for recovering the genuine oneness,

the oneness that has been lost by Christianity! This oneness is all-inclusive; it includes all positive things. Division, on the contrary, includes all negative things. We have seen that when we come back to the oneness, all the godly, heavenly, spiritual things return. The reason is that all these things exist in the oneness. On the one hand, we must admit that we are still quite short and have a long way to go. On the other hand, we can testify that the Lord's riches surely are to be found in His recovery. The unique ground of oneness is here, and all the spiritual riches are included with this ground. All the godly things and all the spiritual riches are ours on the ground of oneness.

THE TESTIMONY OF THE LORD
ON THE GROUND OF ONENESS

The testimony of the Lord today goes along with the recovery of the ground of oneness. This testimony does not depend on our efforts at self-improvement. We may make up our mind to improve ourselves, only to fall once again into failure. The Lord's testimony does not depend on our efforts; it depends on His work within us on the ground of oneness. After we came into the church life, spontaneously the aspiration for godliness, holiness, and spirituality was stirred within us. This was not our own doing; it was altogether the Lord's doing. Because we are on the proper ground, the ground of oneness, the Word of God is transparently open to us. This is wholly due to the Lord's blessing on the ground of oneness. Where the recovery of the ground of oneness is, there the testimony of the Lord is also.

When God's people in the Old Testament returned to Jerusalem, all the things pertaining to God's testimony returned: the altar, the offerings, the temple, the feasts, and the rich enjoyment. However, those who remained in Babylon had nothing to do with the testimony of the Lord. The godly things were found not in Babylon; they were in Jerusalem, the unique place of God's choice. Even though God's returned people were weak or inadequate in many respects, it cannot be denied that the Lord's testimony was with them, not with those in Babylon.

Furthermore, the return of God's people to the ground of

oneness was also used by God to bring forth Christ. Mary, the mother of the Lord Jesus, was a descendant of those who had returned from captivity. If the captives had not returned, there would not have been a way for Christ to be born in Bethlehem. There would have been no channel, no means, for Him to come forth according to the prophecies. Hence, the return from captivity in Babylon was a necessary preparation for the coming of Christ. In the same principle, I believe that the Lord's recovery today will be used by God as a preparation for the Lord's coming back. May the Lord fully use His recovery for the sake of His coming back!

CHAPTER TEN

THE ULTIMATE REVELATION
OF THE LOCAL ONENESS AND ITS RECOVERY

Scripture Reading: Gen. 1:1; Mal. 1:1-2; Matt. 1:1; 16:16-18; 18:17; John 1:1, 14; 20:17; Acts 8:1a; 13:1a; 14:23; 1 Cor. 1:2a; Gal. 1:2; Rev. 1:4-5a, 11, 20; 3:22; 22:17a

In the foregoing chapters we have devoted much attention to various portions of the Old Testament. In this chapter we need to have an overall view of the New Testament concerning the ultimate revelation of the local oneness and its recovery.

A BIRD'S-EYE VIEW OF
THE OLD TESTAMENT REVELATION OF GOD

If we have a bird's-eye view of the Bible and consider the Bible as a whole, we will see that it reveals four main figures. First, the Bible reveals God as the Creator. The very first verse of the Bible, Genesis 1:1, says, "In the beginning God created the heavens and the earth." God was in the beginning, and all things were created by Him. Malachi 1:1 and 2 reveal that this very God is also the One who loves Israel. Hence, the Old Testament reveals God as the Creator of all things and as the One who loves a particular people, Israel. In a sense, this is a summary of the revelation of God in the Old Testament. We may call this God the God of Israel. This term is even used in the Old Testament. The Jews, of course, love the Old Testament very much because it reveals that the unique God in the universe, the One who created the heavens and the earth, is also the very One who loves Israel.

CHRIST AND THE CHURCH

As we all know, the New Testament goes on to reveal much

more of God. For this reason, we who believe in Christ cannot say that the revelation of God in the Old Testament is fully a revelation of our God, for it is actually only a partial and incomplete revelation of Him.

Matthew 1:1 says, "The book of the generation of Jesus Christ, the son of David, the son of Abraham." How different is the opening of the New Testament from the first verse of the Old Testament! The One spoken of in Matthew 1:1 is revealed further in Matthew 16. In this chapter the Lord Jesus asked His disciples, "Who do men say that the Son of Man is?" (v. 13). After the disciples made some reply, the Lord directed His question to them specifically: "But you, who do you say that I am?" (v. 15). Receiving the revelation from the Father in the heavens, Simon Peter answered and said, "You are the Christ, the Son of the living God" (v. 16). The Lord acknowledged that this revelation did not come from flesh and blood but from the Father. Then He went on to say, "You are Peter, and upon this rock I will build My church, and the gates of Hades shall not prevail against it" (v. 18). What we have here is not Israel loved by God—we have the church built by Christ.

John 1:1 says, "In the beginning was the Word, and the Word was with God, and the Word was God." In verse 14 we are told that "the Word became flesh and tabernacled among us...full of grace and reality." This Word who was in the beginning with God and who became flesh is the very God who created all things, but He is much more. In our preaching of the gospel we need to tell our Jewish friends of this. We need to teach them the truth that the God who created all things became a man through incarnation. We must tell them that God did not stop simply with being the One who loved Israel. According to the Gospel of John, He became a man. Hence, to know God only as God is to know Him in an incomplete way.

After living on earth for thirty-three and a half years, Christ was crucified and then entered into resurrection. On the day of His resurrection, Christ said, "Go to My brothers and say to them, I ascend to My Father and your Father, and My God and your God" (20:17). In Matthew we have Christ and the church. In John we have the Son of God and His many brothers, who are the church. After His resurrection Christ began to call the disciples brothers, for through His resurrection they had been regenerated (1 Pet. 1:3) with the divine life released by His life-imparting death, as indicated in John 12:24. He was the Father's only Son, as the Father's individual expression. Now, through His death and resurrection, the Father's only Begotten has become "the Firstborn among many brothers" (Rom. 8:29). His many brothers are the many sons of God and the church (Heb. 2:10-12), as a corporate expression of God the Father in the Son.

At this point we see from the revelation in the Bible three main characters: God, Christ, and the church. God is embodied in Christ, and Christ is expressed through the church. This is the revelation at the end of the Gospels.

THE LOCAL CHURCHES

Now we must proceed from Acts through the book of Revelation. Here we see not only God, Christ, and the church; we also have the churches. In Matthew 16 the Lord said, "I will build My church." This church is the unique, universal church typified by Zion. But just as Zion has many peaks, so the universal church has many local expressions. In Matthew 18, where the Lord spoke of taking a matter to the church, we see one of these local expressions. We may also liken the universal church to a tree and the local churches to the branches of the tree. In Matthew 18 we see one of the branches of this universal tree. Here is a local church to which we can go with our problems. Furthermore, such a church can also deal with certain ones and even cause them to be regarded as Gentiles and tax collectors.

In the book of Acts we read of the church in Jerusalem (8:1) and of another church in Antioch (13:1). According to Acts 14:23, the apostles ordained elders in every church. The churches referred to here are those established in the provinces of Asia Minor. First Corinthians 1:2 speaks of "the church of God which is in Corinth." Furthermore, in Galatians 1:2 Paul refers to "the churches of Galatia," a region of the Roman Empire that included many localities. Just as there are many local churches in the state of California today, so there were a number of churches in the region of Galatia at the time of Paul.

In the book of Revelation the divine revelation in the Bible reaches its consummation. The universal church, as the Body of Christ, is expressed through the local churches. The local churches, as the expressions of the one Body of Christ (1:12, 20), are locally one. Revelation 1:4 says, "John to the seven churches which are in Asia." Asia was a province of the ancient Roman Empire in which were the seven cities mentioned in 1:11. The seven churches were in those seven cities respectively, not all in one city. Revelation does not deal with the universal church but with the local churches in various cities. We have seen that the church is first revealed as universal in Matthew 16:18 and then as local in Matthew 18:17. In Acts the church was practiced in the way of local churches, such as the church in Jerusalem (8:1) and the church in Antioch (13:1) and the churches in the provinces of Syria and Cilicia (15:41). Without the local churches, there is no practicality and actuality of the universal church. The universal church is realized in the local churches. Knowing the church universally must be consummated in knowing the church locally. It is a great advance for us to know and practice the local churches. Concerning the church, the book of Revelation is in the advanced stage, for it is written to local churches. If we would know this book, we must advance from the understanding of the universal church to the realization and practice of the local churches.

ONE CITY, ONE CHURCH

In 1:11 the voice said to John, "What you see write in a scroll and send it to the seven churches: to Ephesus and to Smyrna and to Pergamos and to Thyatira and to Sardis and to Philadelphia and to Laodicea." This verse is composed in a very important way. Here we see that the sending of this book "to the seven churches" equals sending it to the seven cities. This shows clearly that the practice of the church life was that of one church for one city, one city with one church. In no city was there more than one church. The jurisdiction of a local church should cover the whole city in which the church is; it should not be greater or lesser than the boundary of the city. All the believers within that boundary should constitute the unique local church within that city. Hence, one church equals one city, and one city equals one church. This is what we call the local churches.

GRACE AND PEACE FROM THE TRIUNE GOD
TO THE SEVEN CHURCHES

Revelation 1:4 and 5 are very significant verses: "John to the seven churches which are in Asia: Grace to you and peace from Him who is and who was and who is coming, and from the seven Spirits who are before His throne, and from Jesus Christ, the faithful Witness, the Firstborn of the dead, and the Ruler of the kings of the earth." According to these verses, grace and peace are transmitted to the seven churches from the Triune God. Notice that in these verses there are three *from*s: from Him who is and who was and who is coming (the Father); from the seven Spirits (the Spirit); and from Jesus Christ (the Son). What a full, complete revelation of the Triune God! As God the eternal Father, He was in the past, He is in the present, and He is coming in the future. As God the Spirit, He is the sevenfold intensified Spirit for God's operation. As God the Son, He is the Witness, the testimony, the expression of God; the Firstborn of the dead for the church, the new creation; and the Ruler of the kings of the earth for the world. From such a Triune God grace and peace are imparted to the churches.

The revelation of God in these verses is much more complete than the revelation in Genesis 1:1. The God revealed in Genesis could not be called Jesus, for in Genesis we do not yet have the incarnation. According to John 1, the very God who is the Creator in Genesis 1 is the Word who became flesh and tabernacled among us. When the Word became flesh, He was given the name Jesus. In Revelation 1:5 Jesus is the faithful Witness and the Ruler of the kings of the earth. Revelation 1:4 and 5 contain the ultimate revelation in the Bible. The revelation in the Scriptures begins with God as the Creator and consummates with the processed Triune God imparting grace and peace to the local churches. According to Revelation 1:4, the Spirit has become the seven Spirits, that is, the all-inclusive Spirit. Furthermore, the Son has become the faithful Witness, the Firstborn of the dead, and the Ruler of the kings of the

earth. Having passed through incarnation, human living, crucifixion, resurrection, and ascension, He has been enthroned
above all kings. This processed Triune God is related not primarily to individuals or to the church in a general way but to
the churches. For this reason, Revelation 1:4 and 5 specifically
say that grace and peace come from the Triune God to the
seven churches.

THE PROGRESS OF THE DIVINE REVELATION

God's revelation began with God Himself and continued
with Christ and the Spirit until it reached its goal in the local
churches. Without the local churches we do not have the goal
of the divine revelation. Here the shortage among the Jews,
many Christians, and even many so-called spiritual people becomes evident. The Jews have God, most Christians have God
and Christ, and the improved Christians also have the Spirit,
but very few Christians have the proper church life in the local
churches. Today in the local churches we have God, Christ, the
Spirit, and the church.

The issue of the progress of the manifestation of God is the
church. God is embodied in Christ, Christ is realized and experienced as the Spirit who imparts life to us, and the Spirit
issues in the churches. When we experience and realize Christ
as the life-giving Spirit, the issue is the church life. The church
is the Body, the fullness, of Christ. The progress of this revelation is God, Christ, the Spirit, the church, and the local
churches. This is the revelation of God in His holy Word.

In Revelation 22:17 we read a marvelous expression: "The
Spirit and the bride say..." Here we have a compound subject—
the Spirit and the bride. The Spirit is the processed, all-inclusive,
life-giving Triune God, and the bride is the church composed
of all the churches with all the saints. The fact that the Spirit
and the bride speak the same thing indicates that the Triune
God has become utterly one with His redeemed people. How
wonderful!

We need to be deeply impressed with the progress of the
divine revelation in the Bible. We have pointed out that in the
Old Testament we have God as the Creator and as the One
who loves Israel. Then in Matthew and John we read of the

genealogy of Jesus Christ and of the Word becoming flesh and tabernacling among us. Furthermore, in these books we read of the church built by Christ and of the many brothers of the Son of God who are the church. In Acts the church is established in various cities. Most of the Epistles were written to particular local churches. Finally, in the book of Revelation we see that grace and peace are imparted to the local churches from the processed Triune God. Ultimately, according to Revelation 22:17, the Spirit and the bride speak as one, indicating that the Triune God is truly one with His redeemed people.

OUR LOCAL CHURCH

If we are clear about the revelation in the Bible, we will realize that the proper place to enjoy God today is in the local churches. In particular, we need to be in a definite local church that we can say is our local church. Although I love all the churches, I must be honest and testify that no church is as dear and lovable to me as the church in Anaheim because the church in Anaheim is my local church. We should all feel this way about the church in our locality.

How pitiful is the situation of most Christians today! Because they are not in the church life, they are orphans without a home. This was our condition before we came into the church life in the Lord's recovery. Not only were we orphans—we were wanderers. Before we came into the local churches, we never had the sense that we had come home or that we had reached our destination. But the day we came into the church life, we knew that we had come home. After wandering for years, we had finally reached our destination. Something deep within said, "This is the place." Many seeking Christians today, on the contrary, are still travelers; they are traveling from one denomination or group to another. But the day we came into the church life, our wandering ceased. The local churches are what God desires today. This is the last station of His revelation.

All genuine Christians believe that Christ is the very God who created the universe, who became a man, who died on the cross for our redemption, and who was resurrected bodily from among the dead. All real Christians have received this Christ as their Savior and Redeemer. However, it is possible to be such a genuine Christian and still be experientially either in the Gospels or in Acts. We must be Christians in the book of Revelation; that is, we must be those in God's ultimate and consummate revelation. We must be Christians who enjoy the processed, all-inclusive, life-giving Triune God mingled with the churches. If we are in this reality, then we are Christians in Revelation.

It is easy for believers to see the universal church, but it is difficult for them to see the local churches. The revelation of the local churches is the Lord's ultimate unveiling concerning the church. It has been given here in the last book of the divine Word. To fully know the church, believers must follow the Lord from the Gospels, through the Epistles, to the book of Revelation until they are enabled to see the local churches as unveiled here. In Revelation the first vision is concerning the churches. The churches with Christ as their center are the focus in the divine administration for the accomplishment of God's eternal purpose.

We have seen the four main figures revealed in the Bible: God, Christ, the church, and the churches. Our God is not merely the Creator in Genesis 1. He is the processed God in Revelation 1:4 and 5. He is the One who is and who was and who is coming; He is the seven Spirits; and He is Jesus Christ, the faithful Witness, the Firstborn of the dead, and the Ruler of the kings of the earth. How blessed we are to know God in this way and to have such a bird's-eye view of the Bible! What a privilege to hear such a word concerning the ultimate revelation of God in the Scriptures! Today in our local church we can enjoy the processed, all-inclusive, life-giving Triune God.

THE SPIRIT SPEAKING TO THE CHURCHES

In Revelation 2 and 3 we are told again and again that the Spirit speaks to the churches. This is very different from the Old Testament expression *Thus says Jehovah*. Since the Spirit today is speaking to the churches, we must be in one of the local churches in order to hear His speaking. The Spirit today is speaking directly to the churches. Therefore, it is vital for us to be in one of the churches, in a church that we can designate as our local church.

GOLDEN LAMPSTANDS

In Revelation the churches, signified by the golden lampstands, are the testimony of Jesus (1:2, 9) in the divine nature, shining in the dark night locally yet collectively. The churches should be of the divine nature—golden. They should be the stands, even the lampstands, that bear the lamp with the oil (Christ as the life-giving Spirit), shining in the darkness respectively and collectively. They are individual lampstands locally, yet at the same time they are a group, a collection, of lampstands universally. They are not only shining locally but also bearing universally the same testimony both to the localities and to the universe. They are of the same nature and in the same shape. They bear the same lamp for the same purpose and are fully identified with one another, not having any individual distinctiveness. The differences of the local churches recorded in chapters 2 and 3 are all of a negative nature, not of a positive nature. Negatively, in their failures they are different and separate one from another; but positively, in their nature, shape, and purpose they are absolutely identical and connected one to another.

IMPLYING THE SIGNIFICANCE OF THE TRIUNE GOD

Throughout the centuries few Christians have touched the depths of the significance of the lampstands as symbols of the local churches. According to our natural concept, a lampstand is simply an object holding a lamp that shines in the darkness. The lampstand in Exodus 25 is pure gold, and the lampstands in Zechariah 4 and Revelation also are golden. Substantially, the lampstand is golden. With the lampstand we see three important things: the gold, the stand, and the lamps. The lampstand implies the significance of the Triune God. Gold is the substance with which the lampstand is made, the stand is the embodiment of the gold, and the lamps are the expression of the stand. The gold signifies the Father as the substance, the stand signifies the Son as the embodiment of the Father, and the lamps signify the Spirit as the expression of the Father in the Son. Thus, the significance of the Triune God is implied in the lampstand. Substantially, the lampstand is one, but expressively, it is seven because it is one lampstand with seven lamps. At the bottom the lampstand is one; at the top, it is seven. Should we argue about whether it is one or seven? In substance the lampstand is one piece of gold, but it holds seven lamps. This mysteriously indicates that substantially the Triune God is one. In substance He is one, but in expression He is the seven Spirits. The Father as the substance is embodied in the Son as the form, and the Son is expressed as the seven Spirits.

How can we prove that the seven lamps are the Spirit expressing Christ? The seven lamps are first mentioned in Exodus. If we only had the record in Exodus, however, it would be difficult to realize that these seven lamps are the Spirit. But as we proceed from Exodus to Zechariah, we see that the seven lamps are the seven eyes of Christ and the seven eyes of God (Zech. 3:9; 4:10). As we continue on to Revelation, we see that the seven eyes of the Lamb are the seven Spirits, which are the intensified Spirit of God. Hence, we have a strong basis for saying that the seven lamps are the sevenfold intensified Spirit as the expression of Christ.

THE TRIUNE GOD EMBODIED AND EXPRESSED

We have seen that the lampstand implies the significance of the Triune God; it symbolizes the Triune God embodied and expressed. God the Father as the divine gold is embodied in Christ the Son and then is fully expressed through the Spirit. The expression differs from the embodiment. The embodiment must be uniquely one because our God is uniquely one. Thus, the embodiment must be one stand. The expression, however, must be complete, and it must be complete in God's move. Recall that seven is the number for completion in God's move. Throughout the centuries God has been expressed in His move. This is the reason that the seven lamps signify the intensified Spirit as the expression of Christ in God's complete move. This is the practical understanding of the Trinity.

The Trinity is for the dispensing of God into humanity. God, the Divine Being, is first embodied in Christ and then expressed through the sevenfold intensified Spirit. Now we have not only the Triune God; in the lampstand we have the Triune God substantially and solidly embodied and expressed. The gold has been formed into the solid stand. It once was just gold, but now it is the stand. The gold has been formed into a stand for the fulfillment of God's purpose. Without the stand there is no way for God's purpose to be fulfilled. As we have seen, this stand, which is a type of Christ, is expressed through the seven lamps signifying the seven Spirits of God. The seven Spirits of God are not separate from God; they are the seven eyes of God and of the Lamb, the Redeemer. They are also the seven eyes of the building stone (Zech. 3:9). Hence, they are the seven eyes with the redemption of Christ for God's building. Whenever these eyes look at people, people are redeemed and built into God's house.

THE REPRODUCTION
OF CHRIST AND THE SPIRIT

In Exodus 25 the emphasis is on the stand, in Zechariah 4 the emphasis is on the lamps, and in Revelation 1 the emphasis is on the reproduction. In both Exodus and Zechariah the lampstand is one, but in Revelation it has been reproduced and has become seven. First, in Exodus the emphasis is on the stand—on Christ. Second, in Zechariah the emphasis is on the lamps—on the Spirit. Eventually, in Revelation both the stand and lamps, that is, both Christ and the Spirit, are reproduced as the churches. In Exodus and Zechariah there are just seven lamps, but here in Revelation there are forty-nine lamps, for every lampstand has seven lamps. Hence, the one lampstand has become seven, and the seven lamps have become forty-nine. The lampstands with their lamps in Revelation are the reproduction of Christ and the Spirit. When Christ is realized, He is the Spirit, and when the Spirit is realized, we have the churches as the reproduction.

SUBSTANCE, EXISTENCE, AND EXPRESSION

The church is not only universally one but also expressed locally in many cities. In the whole universe there is only one Christ, one Spirit, and one church. There are the seven churches because of the need for an expression. For existence, one is sufficient, but for expression, many are needed. If we would know the church, we must know its substance, existence, and expression. Substantially, the church, and even all the churches, are one. In expression, the many churches are the many lampstands. What is the church? The church is the expression of the Triune God, and this expression is seen in many localities on earth. The church is signified not by just one lampstand but by seven lampstands. In Revelation 1 there are seven lampstands with forty-nine lamps shining in the universe. This is the testimony of Jesus.

The church is the testimony of Jesus. This means that the church is the expression of the Triune God substantially and expressively. Substantially, it is of one substance in the whole universe; expressively, it is many lampstands with the lamps shining in the darkness to express the Triune God. The Father as the substance is embodied in the Son, the Son as the embodiment is expressed through the Spirit, the Spirit is fully realized and reproduced as the churches, and the churches are the testimony of Jesus. If we see this vision, it will govern us, and we will never be divisive.

We have seen that the lampstand is the divine gold embodied in a substantial form to fulfill God's purpose in His move. The expression of the stand is in the shining of the light. As the expression shines, the shining fulfills God's eternal purpose. Thus, the lampstand signifies not only the Triune God but also the move of the Triune God in His embodiment and expression. We have also seen that the local churches are the reproduction of the embodiment and expression of the Triune God. We should not be satisfied with saying that the local churches are the lampstands shining in the dark night. Although this is correct, it is rather shallow. We must see that the local churches are the reproduction of the embodiment and expression of the Triune God.

IN THE LOCAL CHURCH
ON THE GROUND OF ONENESS

We have pointed out that when God's people in the Old Testament lost the ground of oneness, they spontaneously lost so many spiritual and holy things. However, when they returned to Jerusalem, to the ground of oneness, all these holy and spiritual things spontaneously returned. The principle is the same in the Lord's recovery today. Today our God, the Triune God, is the Father embodied in the Son and the Son realized as the all-inclusive Spirit. Today this Spirit is speaking to the churches. Hence, in order to hear the Spirit's speaking, we must be in one of the churches. Eventually, the Spirit and the bride, constituted of all the churches with all the saints, will be one and will speak with one voice. Today we are listening to the speaking of the Spirit. But the day is coming when together the Spirit and the bride will say, "Come!" Praise the Lord for this vision! With such a clear vision in front of us, we know where we must be today—in the local oneness, that is, in the local church on the ground of oneness.

If we are not in the local oneness, we are not in the church in a genuine and practical way. Furthermore, we cannot have the full experience of the processed, all-inclusive Triune God. The reason many Christians today are in spiritual poverty is that they have neither the genuine oneness nor the full experience of the all-inclusive Spirit. They have the Bible, but they do not have much experience of Christ as life. They have the name of Christ, but they have very little reality of His person. So many spiritual things are lacking because the ground of oneness has been damaged and even lost. Only on this ground can we have the full experience of the processed Triune God. Remember, the dispensation of the Triune God, according to Revelation 1:4 and 5, is to local churches.

THE GROUND OF LOCALITY

The ground of oneness about which we have been speaking is the ground of locality. More than twenty years ago in Taipei, a certain Christian from America, an intimate friend of ours, was our family physician. Although he heard me deliver thirty messages concerning the ground of the church, he told me one day that he simply was not able to understand this matter of the ground of locality. I explained this to him very carefully, but still he did not understand it. Eventually, he admitted that he had some understanding of the ground of oneness but not of the ground of locality.

Brother T. Austin-Sparks had the same difficulty. Many years ago he and I had about twenty long conversations, lasting two or three hours each, regarding the ground of the church. At one point he told me that he was not able to understand this term, *the ground of locality*. I pointed out to him that, as he no doubt realized, the children of Israel were allowed to build the temple only on one particular site, on Mount Moriah, where Abraham had offered his son Isaac. That unique site was the ground on which the temple was built. That ground preserved the oneness of God's people. I went on to say that God's people were not allowed to build a temple in Babylon, even if the temple would have been the same in size and design as the original temple in Jerusalem. A temple constructed in Babylon could not have been the center of oneness. On the contrary, such a temple would have been a center of division. All those who returned from captivity were required to go back to the ground of oneness, to Mount Zion, where the temple was rebuilt. Hence, the temple on Mount Zion was built on the ground of oneness. This portrays the genuine oneness of believers today, a oneness on the proper ground, on the ground of locality. I believe that Mr. Austin-Sparks understood this but was not willing to admit it. Actually, it is not difficult to understand what is meant by the ground of locality. The reason many have difficulty with this is that they are not willing to give up their concept.

THE NEED TO BE
IN THE LOCAL ONENESS

According to the book of Revelation, the oneness of the believers in Christ is a local oneness. Anyone who is not in the local oneness is not actually in the oneness at all. Those who are not in a local church are not truly in the church. In order to be in the church we must be in a local church. In the same principle, if we would be in the oneness, we must be in the local oneness, in the practical oneness in our locality. The local oneness is very practical and personal. If you are not personally in this oneness, you are not really in the oneness, and you are not actually in the church. For this reason, in the title of this chapter we spoke of the ultimate revelation of the local oneness. How we praise the Lord for the revelation and recovery of this oneness!

THE RECOVERY OF THE CHURCH LIFE

This local oneness was damaged and altogether lost by the time the Catholic Church was formed. The emperor Constantine the Great initiated the formation of the Catholic Church early in the fourth century. In A.D. 325 he called a council at Nicaea to settle theological disputes, which were a cause of strife throughout his empire. He used his political influence to bring about a certain kind of unity. By the end of the sixth century the Catholic Church was fully formed with the establishment of the papal system. At that time the local oneness was absolutely destroyed and lost.

During the following centuries, a period known as the Dark Ages, the Bible was locked away from the people, and the truth of salvation was obscured. Then with the Reformation the Bible was released in the language of the people, and the truth of justification by faith was recovered. In the matter of justification, Martin Luther was bold. However, in the matter of the church, he was cowardly. He was even instrumental in the formation of the state church in Germany. The first state church was that formed in Germany through the assistance of Luther. Luther not only made such a terrible blunder, but he persecuted those believers who emphasized the experience of life. For example, Schwenckfeld was called a devil. In the decades that followed, many faithful ones were persecuted and even martyred for their faith, sometimes at the hand of the state churches that had been established in a number of European countries.

THE RECOVERY
IN THE EIGHTEENTH CENTURY

Early in the eighteenth century a number of believers fled to Bohemia to escape persecution. Zinzendorf had both the love and the burden to care for these refugees. However, among them there were disputes over doctrine and practice. When these disputes made it impossible for the believers to go on together peacefully, Zinzendorf required all the leaders to sign a statement that they would set aside their differences and live together in oneness. During the next meeting for the Lord's table, they experienced a mighty outpouring of the Spirit. In this way the practice of the church life was recovered, at least in a beginning way.

THE RECOVERY WITH THE BRETHREN

Another kind of reaction to religious formality and deadness was that of mystics such as Madame Guyon and Father Fenelon. Although this reaction took place in the seventeenth century, there was no recovery of the church life until the eighteenth century. The practice of the church life under the leadership of Zinzendorf was very good, but it was not adequate. Therefore, early in the nineteenth century the Lord took a further step toward the recovery of the church life with a group of believers in Great Britain, especially those with John Nelson Darby. For approximately twenty-five years the Brethren under the leadership of Darby experienced a wonderful recovery of the church life, a recovery that was more complete and adequate than that under Zinzendorf a century earlier. However, due to debates over doctrine, the oneness was lost, and the Brethren were divided. As the years went by, the Brethren were divided into more than a hundred divisions. Because the oneness was so seriously damaged, the presence of the Lord with them was greatly diminished.

THE RECOVERY IN CHINA

In the 1920s the Lord raised up a group of young people in China under the leadership of Watchman Nee. Brother Nee once told me that the Lord was forced to come to China because, as far as the practice of the church life was concerned, China was still virgin soil, whereas the United States and Europe had been spoiled. There was no way for the Lord to have a proper start for the church life in either Europe or the United States. Therefore, He sowed the seed of the recovery of the church life in the virgin soil of China.

The first church established in the Lord's recovery was raised up in 1922 in Foochow, Brother Nee's hometown. After I was saved in 1925, I came in contact with Brother Nee through his writings. His writings helped a number of us to see the mistakes of the denominations. We came to realize that although we held to the Lord's name, the gospel, and the Bible, we had to drop many other aspects of organized Christianity. Under the leadership of Brother Nee, we studied church history, biographies, and all the important spiritual and doctrinal writings. Through our study we gained a detailed knowledge of Christianity. Gradually, we came to discern those practices that we should adopt: immersion, eldership, practical holiness, and the proper Pentecostal spirituality. Those who visited our meetings were often troubled by the fact that they could not categorize us. To some we appeared to be like Baptists, but to others we resembled the Presbyterians or the Plymouth Brethren.

In 1932 the church was raised up in my hometown, Chefoo. We did not know how to practice the church life. We only knew that we loved the Lord Jesus and that we could not agree with traditional Christianity. We came together simply with a heart for the Lord and with the Bible. We did not know how to meet, in particular how to have the Lord's table. Nevertheless, we enjoyed the sweetness of the Lord's presence.

THE BOUNDARY OF LOCALITY

In 1930 Brother Nee visited Europe, Canada, and the United States. During the course of his visit, he saw the confusion and the divisiveness among the Brethren assemblies. Troubled by the situation, he resolved to re-study the New Testament concerning the boundary of a local assembly. Through this study he saw that the boundary of a local assembly must be the boundary of that locality in which that assembly is. This truth of the boundary of locality was put forth in *The Assembly Life*. In this book Brother Nee placed strong emphasis on what he called the local border.

THE LOCAL GROUND

In 1937 he saw further light regarding the local oneness of the church. From the local border he went on to see the local ground. Calling an urgent meeting of the co-workers, he delivered the messages published later in *The Normal Christian*

Church Life. This book emphasizes the local ground. By 1937 the matter of the local oneness was fully recovered among us. We became utterly clear that the practice of the church life requires us to be on the local ground, that is, on the ground of oneness.

Since this matter of the ground of locality was recovered, a number of Christians have argued with us concerning it. Some have said, "In saying that you are the local church, you are proud. How can you say that you are the church and that we are not? You claim to be the church in Shanghai. Are we not the church in Shanghai also?" At first we were troubled by such criticism. We did not have the experience to deal with it. Later, by contending for the truth of oneness, we learned how to deal with the various criticisms, objections, and arguments.

AN EFFECTIVE ILLUSTRATION
OF THE LOCAL ONENESS

If someone tries to argue with you concerning the ground of oneness, point as an illustration to the situation of the children of Israel in the land of Canaan. Jerusalem was the unique place, the unique center, chosen by God to maintain the oneness of His people. Eventually, God's people were carried away into captivity, some to Egypt, others to Assyria, and still others to Babylon. Originally, God's people were one, with a unique center of worship on Mount Zion in Jerusalem. But they became scattered into at least three major divisions. After the seventy years of captivity in Babylon had expired, God commanded the people to return to Jerusalem. A remnant of the people did return. By returning to Jerusalem, they spontaneously formed a fourth group among God's people. Before the return from captivity, there were just three groups—those in Egypt, Assyria, and Babylon. Although these three groups were divisions, the fourth group, constituted of those who had returned to Jerusalem, was not a division. Yes, the fourth group was a distinct group, but it was a recovery, not a division.

Perhaps some of God's people who chose to remain in Babylon said, "Brothers, you shouldn't be so narrow. God is everywhere. We don't need to go back to Jerusalem to worship Him. Consider Daniel. He loved the Lord and served Him without going back to Jerusalem. If he could stay in Babylon, then we are free to do the same thing." Under the Lord's sovereignty, Daniel remained in Babylon even after the year Cyrus issued the decree ordering the captives to return to Jerusalem (2 Chron. 36:22; Dan. 1:21; 10:1). Prior to that time, Daniel prayed daily with his windows opened toward Jerusalem. This indicates that Daniel desired to go back to Jerusalem; however, he was not given the opportunity to do so. Therefore, his case should not be used as an excuse to remain in Babylon, that is, to stay in division.

For God's people to remain in Egypt, Assyria, or Babylon was to remain in division. Those who returned to Jerusalem did not cause further division. On the contrary, they shared in the recovery of the genuine oneness. Among the four groups, only they could be regarded as the nation of Israel. Although the ones who remained in Babylon may have vastly outnumbered those who returned to Jerusalem, those who returned could be regarded as the nation of Israel, whereas those who remained could not.

In principle, the same is true with respect to the nation of Israel today. It is those who have returned to the good land who are recognized as the nation of Israel, not those who are still scattered throughout the world. For example, the number of Jews in New York City may exceed the number of those in Israel. Nevertheless, as even the United Nations recognizes, the Jews in Israel make up the nation of Israel, whereas the Jews in New York do not. Those in New York may love the nation of Israel and may give generously to support it. Nevertheless, simply because they have not returned to the land of their fathers, they cannot be regarded as the nation of Israel. To be part of the nation of Israel one must be not only a Jew—he must be a Jew on the proper ground, that is, in the good land.

THOSE WHO CONSTITUTE THE CHURCH

We may apply the principle contained in this illustration to the situation concerning the church today. When we take the standing that we are the church in Anaheim, other Christians may protest. They may ask, "How can you say that you are the church in Anaheim and that we are not?" If someone raises this question, find out where he is. Check to see if he is in a denomination or some other divisive group of Christians. If he is in a division, then in a practical sense he is not part of the church in his locality. Many of today's Christians are like Jews who have not returned to the land of Israel. Only those Jews who have returned to the original ground of oneness, to the land of their fathers, are part of the nation of Israel. In the same principle, to be part of the local church one must not only be a Christian but must also be a Christian on the ground of oneness. Only those believers who have forsaken every divisive ground and have come back to the ground of oneness constitute the church. No matter how few they may be in number, those who have returned to the ground of oneness are the church in their locality.

If we who meet on the ground of oneness in Anaheim are not the church in Anaheim, what are we? I ask those who dispute our testimony concerning the church to give us a name. The fact is, we do not have a name. We simply meet together as the church in our locality.

When speaking of the ground of oneness, learn to use the illustration of the return of the children of Israel from captivity. Also point to the situation of the nation of Israel today. Many of the Jews in New York City may be better Jews than those in Palestine. Nevertheless, because those in Palestine are on the proper ground, they are the nation of Israel. In like manner, the Christians who have returned to the ground of oneness are the church, not necessarily because they are more spiritual than others but because they have come back to the proper ground, to the ground of oneness.

PAYING THE PRICE
TO STAND ON THE GROUND OF ONENESS

Do you know why many of God's people remained in Babylon instead of making the long journey back to Jerusalem? The reason was that they were settled comfortably in Babylon and did not want to pay the price to return to the good land. The same holds true of many Jews in the United States today. They may be very devoted to the nation of Israel, but they find it inconvenient to move there to be part of that nation. Having a settled place in American society, they may prefer to be American Jews. This indicates that they are not willing to pay the price to stand on the unique ground. Sorry to say, the same thing is true of many Christians. A number of them have seen something of the truth of oneness. But the problem is they are not willing to pay the price. Returning to the ground of oneness would cause many to lose their position, name, reputation, or popularity. By the Lord's mercy, we have chosen to take the narrow way of the cross and to stand on the ground of oneness. We have no choice except to take the Lord's choice, even though we may be defamed, despised, and criticized. We must pay the price to stand on the ground of local oneness no matter what evil things others may say about us.

Praise the Lord for all the spiritual and heavenly things that have become our experience on this ground! Here in the local, unique oneness we have the Lord's presence, the altar, the house, and the feasts. Nothing can compare with the enjoyment of the spiritual riches on the proper ground. How happy I am to be with you all in the local oneness! Unless the Lord leads us to make a genuine migration to another locality, we should simply remain in our local church, not moving to suit our taste or preference. Let us simply stay in the church where the Lord has placed us. We praise the Lord for the vision concerning the destruction of the high places and the recovery of the local oneness. Hallelujah for the revelation of the local oneness and its recovery! It is our privilege to have a share in this recovery today.

ABOUT THE AUTHOR

Witness Lee was born in 1905 in northern China and raised in a Christian family. At age 19 he was fully captured for Christ and immediately consecrated himself to preach the gospel for the rest of his life. Early in his service, he met Watchman Nee, a renowned preacher, teacher, and writer. Witness Lee labored together with Watchman Nee under his direction. In 1934 Watchman Nee entrusted Witness Lee with the responsibility for his publication operation, called the Shanghai Gospel Bookroom.

Prior to the Communist takeover in 1949, Witness Lee was sent by Watchman Nee and his other co-workers to Taiwan to ensure that the things delivered to them by the Lord would not be lost. Watchman Nee instructed Witness Lee to continue the former's publishing operation abroad as the Taiwan Gospel Bookroom, which has been publicly recognized as the publisher of Watchman Nee's works outside China. Witness Lee's work in Taiwan manifested the Lord's abundant blessing. From a mere 350 believers, newly fled from the mainland, the churches in Taiwan grew to 20,000 in five years.

In 1962 Witness Lee felt led of the Lord to come to the United States, and he began to minister in Los Angeles. During his 35 years of service in the U.S., he ministered in weekly meetings and weekend conferences, delivering several thousand spoken messages. Much of his speaking has since been published as over 400 titles. Many of these have been translated into over fourteen languages. He gave his last public conference in February 1997 at the age of 91.

He leaves behind a prolific presentation of the truth in the Bible. His major work, *Life-study of the Bible,* comprises over 25,000 pages of commentary on every book of the Bible from the perspective of the believers' enjoyment and experience of God's divine life in Christ through the Holy Spirit. Witness Lee was the chief editor of a new translation of the New Testament into Chinese called the Recovery Version and directed the translation of the same into English. The Recovery Version also appears in a number of other languages. He provided an extensive body of footnotes, outlines, and spiritual cross references. A radio broadcast of his messages can be heard on Christian radio stations in the United States. In 1965 Witness Lee founded Living Stream Ministry, a non-profit corporation, located in Anaheim, California, which officially presents his and Watchman Nee's ministry.

Witness Lee's ministry emphasizes the experience of Christ as life and the practical oneness of the believers as the Body of Christ. Stressing the importance of attending to both these matters, he led the churches under his care to grow in Christian life and function. He was unbending in his conviction that God's goal is not narrow sectarianism but the Body of Christ. In time, believers began to meet simply as the church in their localities in response to this conviction. In recent years a number of new churches have been raised up in Russia and in many European countries.

OTHER BOOKS PUBLISHED BY
Living Stream Ministry

Titles by Witness Lee:

Titles by Watchman Nee:

Available at
Christian bookstores, or contact Living Stream Ministry
2431 W. La Palma Ave. • Anaheim, CA 92801
1-800-549-5164 • www.livingstream.com